PRAISE FOR *COMMANDO DAD:*

COMMANDO DAD

FOREST SCHOOL ADVENTURES

GET OUTDOORS WITH YOUR KIDS

NEIL SINCLAIR

DEDICATION

To our three troopers, Sam, Jude and Liberty. Although you're now a little too old for the adventures contained here, your dad is sure we have lots of other adventures to look forward to.

ABOUT THE AUTHOR

Photograph © Kate Waldock

Neil Sinclair is an ex-commando, qualified Forest School Practitioner, and was a stay-at-home dad for 14 years. He has three amazing children and lives in the Lake District.

CONTENTS

INTRODUCTION

To Dads, Carers and other Forest Adventurers—this book is for YOU.

Can you remember a time when your life seemed full of possibilities, magic and opportunities for adventure? You can? Think about where you were when you had those feelings. I'm willing to bet you were outside—running around and feeling the freedom and excitement that come with simply being in the natural world.

When I was a boy, my parents were Salvation Army officers, which meant moving every three years, always to an urban environment, always to a house without a garden. So my brothers and I sought out natural surroundings whenever we could: the park, wasteland, local woods, the beach. We instinctively knew there was something special about these places, because even when we were playing the same games, they seemed somehow *better* outdoors.

We were right. Research has now shown that being around trees and green spaces has real, quantifiable health benefits, both mental and physical. So much so that in some countries outdoor activities are being trialled as prescriptions for medical patients. Being in nature is so good for you, you might one day be able to get it on prescription from your doctor!

But the benefits are not limited to the physical and mental resilience of your unit. There is yet another advantage to the activities in this book: *education*. One of the reasons troopers love being in the great outdoors is because it is thrilling to be in an environment with fewer boundaries and controls, where they can explore freely. They can take risks (supported by you, of course) and increase confidence in their own abilities. They can learn more about themselves and build their self-esteem in the process.

I have maintained my love of the natural world and it has led me on many adventures—one of which was training as a Forest School practitioner. Forest School is a child-centered, holistic learning process: troopers are supported to play and explore in natural environments and learn personal, social and technical skills. I can't recommend it highly enough. If you or your troopers are given an opportunity to take part in a Forest School, grab it! This book is in no way intended as a guidebook for Forest School, but I wanted to recognize the educational nature of all the activities in this book—encouraging skills as diverse as creativity, concentration, communication, dexterity, empathy, hand–eye coordination, independence, perseverance, problem-solving, observation, teamwork and resilience.

Now, to go back to my original question, can you remember a time when your life seemed full of possibilities, magic and opportunities for adventure? That time for your trooper is now. And you can recapture that feeling, or perhaps experience it for the first time. It's as easy as getting out into nature with your troopers, reconnecting with your place in the natural world and daring to learn alongside them in the world's greatest classroom: the great outdoors.

Happy adventuring!

HOW TO USE *COMMANDO DAD: FOREST SCHOOL ADVENTURES*:

Commando Dad: Forest School Adventures is like my other books, in that it is designed to be used by dads "in the field" when you are actively engaged in adventuring with troopers. I have done my best to include a wide range of activities suitable for troopers from age three onwards. However, you know the interests and abilities of your troopers and may find that some of these are suitable for adventurers outside of this age range. Just remember to employ your Commando Dad common sense to keep your troopers engaged—and safe.

This book does differ from my other titles in one important respect: the activities are led by your troopers. While you establish physical and behavioral boundaries (see note on trooper boundary briefs below), your troopers set the pace. This has made it difficult for me to give you an idea of how long activities will take (sometimes an activity will engage your troopers for hours, sometimes for minutes—be prepared).

You might start with one activity and your troopers will take it in another direction. As long as there is no issue with safety, go with it. Adventure together.

Remember to ask open-ended questions (questions without right or wrong answers) to encourage your troopers' curiosity, creativity, reasoning and thinking skills. As you chat, you will be helping them develop their speech and language skills and increase their own confidence in their ability to express themselves in words.

Examples of open-ended questions include:

- What do you think that sound is?
- What do you think made that hole?
- Why do you think it's that shape?

Always give your trooper your undivided attention and let them know how interested you are in their answers. Give them time to fully answer your questions, without interruption, and, importantly, let your trooper decide when they want to change the subject.

If your trooper asks you something that you don't know the answer to, congratulate them on coming up with such a clever question and say you'll find out together later. Then make sure you do—it will be a lovely follow-up activity.

KITBAG:

I provide kit lists for every activity contained in this book. These will supplement your dedicated kitbag of essential supplies, which you will need to keep up to speed and squared away. When adventure comes calling, you need to be ready. I advocate using a backpack with outside pockets because they are roomy enough to fit in what you need, are comfortable to carry, easy to access and leave your arms free for your Commando Dad duties.

Your dedicated kitbag should contain:

- Snacks and water
- Wipes
- Sun block
- Change of clothes and dry socks
- Basic first-aid kit

- ○ Sachets of paediatric paracetamol and paediatric ibuprofen. Check the label to ensure your trooper meets the weight and age requirements before administering
- ○ A selection of plasters, the brighter the better
- ○ Bandage and tape
- ○ Finger bandage
- ○ Antiseptic cream, suitable for stings and bites
- ○ Antiseptic wipes
- ○ Antibacterial hand gel
- ○ Tweezers
- ○ Scissors
- Plastic bags (multiple uses—for trash, for sitting on, for wet clothes, for keeping kit dry, etc.)

CLOTHES:

- Wear clothes that both you and your troopers will happily get dirty. Nothing will kill the sense of freedom quicker than having to worry about staying clean—this is the great outdoors. It's where dirt is born.
- To minimize bites, stings and scratches:
  - ○ Wear long pants and tuck them into socks, boots or rubber boots.
  - ○ Wear long-sleeved tops.
- Keep a hat handy to keep both sun and rain off faces

STANDARD OPERATING PROCEDURES (SOPs):

For Commando Dads:

- Trooper boundary briefs: before any activity, give every trooper a boundary brief, so they understand what is safe to do and what is not. To check their understanding, ask the trooper to explain the rules back to you. Make sure troopers know that it is always OK to ask questions and to check when they're not sure what they should be doing. The idea is to set boundaries so that your troopers remain safe, but don't make them so restrictive that they don't have the freedom to explore.

- Always give your undivided attention (no phones).

- Always remain patient, encouraging and upbeat.

For Troopers:

- Ask questions if you are unsure.

- Do not eat anything you find in the woods without checking with Commando Dad.

- Don't touch mini-beasts (bugs and other small creatures).

- If you're not sure which plants sting, check with Commando Dad before you touch them.

- Know where the rally point is (see below).

- If you hear "One-Two-Three . . . Back to Me!," stop what you are doing and go to the rally point.

- Learn how to handle all tools and knives correctly and safely.

- After every activity, wash your hands with antibacterial hand gel.

- When you get back to base camp, always wash your hands with soap and warm water.

Rally Point:

Determine the "rally point," the point at which the day's activities will begin and end. Make sure the troopers know that if ever they hear Commando Dad shout "One-Two-Three... Back to Me!" they must stop whatever activity they are doing and return to the rally point. It is always worth testing this a couple of times to make sure the troopers understand this important rule.

Mission Key:

Every adventure in this book comes with a mission key indicating difficulty (boot symbol), expense (dollar symbol) and age suitability. They look like this:

SECTION 1:

EXPLORE

This section contains activities to undertake when you and your troopers are exploring the great outdoors.

Troopers are born explorers and will naturally use all their senses to discover the world around them. They will find the natural environment stimulating and engaging—and because it is ever-changing, there is always something exciting to discover. These include new sounds, new smells, new things to touch and feel, and, when you let them, new things to taste. Your role is to set some boundaries and let your troopers explore. See what they do on their own, without suggestions from you. If you want to see the world through their eyes—and I would recommend that you do—let them take the lead and explore *with* them.

ALPHABET EXPLORERS

Mission brief

- **Ground**: wood or forest
- **Situation**: you're making your way to the adventure area for the day's activities
- **Mission**: to be immersed in the natural environment
- **Skills**: observation, communication, imagination

MISSION KEY

$ $ $ $ $ AGES 3+

KIT LIST:

- None

The beauty of this activity is that it encourages troopers to explore the natural environment from the outset, noticing the sights, sounds and smells of the natural environment.

INSTRUCTIONS:

1. When you are walking through the wood/forest, begin the game by saying "I spy with my little eye, something beginning with 'A.'"

2. Troopers have to find something in the natural environment beginning with that letter.

3. If you're walking with a group of troopers, decide whether you want every trooper to find something beginning with A, or whether you're happy to move straight onto B.

4. Stop playing when you get to the area you've designated for the day's adventures.

5. You can resume the game on the way out of the wood/forest if you want to— but be warned, some letters are easier than others!

MISSION ACCOMPLISHED

I verify that on this date .... I completed a game of Alphabet Explorers with my Commando Dad.

Signed:

HUNT FOR MINI-BEASTS

Mission brief

- **Ground:** woods, forest or park
- **Situation:** mini-beasts (bugs and other small creatures) will be easier to find in spring and summer
- **Mission:** to track and identify—but not touch or capture—mini-beasts
- **Skills:** observation, recognition, nature appreciation

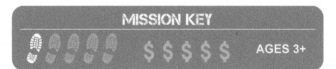

MISSION KEY

$ $ $ $ $ AGES 3+

KIT LIST:

- A camera so you and your troopers can continue to study mini-beasts at base camp

- Paper and pencil for artistic troopers (ideally with something to lean on, such as a clipboard)

- A chart that shows the wildlife you're likely to find in your local woodland, or the area where you're going to be hunting. This can be useful beforehand to prepare the troopers, and later when they are reviewing their photos/pictures

  - You can find great, downloadable "spotting sheets" for British wildlife, sorted by season and habitat, at **www.**

wildlifewatch.org.uk/spotting-sheets—or your troopers can make their own. International readers can search online for "wildlife spotting sheet" and find results more specific to your geographic location

○ You can find an example spotting sheet on pages 22–23

○ Put your spotting sheets in plastic wallets to keep them clean and dry

• Binoculars if you have them; they are not strictly necessary for mini-beasts but will be popular nonetheless

• A magnifying glass if you have one. Avoid using them directly on mini-beasts on sunny days as you will burn them

• Insect repellent if your local wood or park is a haven for swarms of biting insects

• If you're away from base camp, wipes or hand sanitizer to clean hands after hunting mini-beasts

INSTRUCTIONS:

(1) Make sure everyone knows not to touch the mini-beasts.

(2) **Adopt quiet and slow "David Attenborough" tones and encourage the troopers to do the same.** This will have no effect on the bugs whatsoever, but will avoid startling other kinds of wildlife, and will add to the anticipation.

(3) **Move slowly and carefully, making no sudden movements.**

(4) **Be prepared for squeals of disgust and delight.**

(5) **If you're anxious, don't show it.** Troopers take their cues from you, and if you show you're nervous around mini-beasts they will learn to be too.

(6) If you find a mini-beast that could bite or sting, explain to your troopers that it is the creature's natural defence mechanism.

(7) **Challenge misconceptions about mini-beasts.** Bees aren't just stinging machines, they're arch pollinators and without them many plants and crops (including the ones we eat) would die. Flies can be a pain, but they are busy workers in the garden, pollinating, helping to dispose of decaying waste and serving as a protein-rich meal for birds, frogs, spiders and other insects. Worms aren't slimy mini-snakes; they're "nature's ploughs" turning waste into nutrient-rich soil. Dung beetles mean that the world isn't covered in poo!

---

i **NOTE**

Use the mini-beast "spot it" sheet on pages 22–23 to help record what your troopers find.

Mini-beasts are more active in spring and summer, but it is possible to find them all year round, if you know where to look—and you look carefully. Good places to look for mini-beasts in woodland include:

- In or near any kind of flowers or plants
- On leaves
- In or near any kind of shelter, including cracks in tree bark, piles of deadwood or leaves
- In long grass
- In a hedge or bush
- Under large stones and logs, but don't forget your trooper boundary brief—let Commando Dad do any heavy lifting
- In or near any source of water, but don't forget your trooper boundary brief— no trooper goes anywhere near water unless Commando Dad is there and he has said it is OK
- Once your mini-beast hunt is complete, don't forget to thoroughly wash your hands

MINI-BEAST "SPOT IT" SHEET

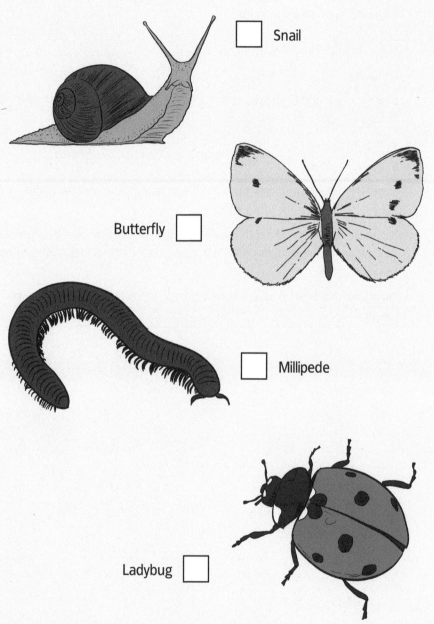

Snail ☐

Butterfly ☐

Millipede ☐

Ladybug ☐

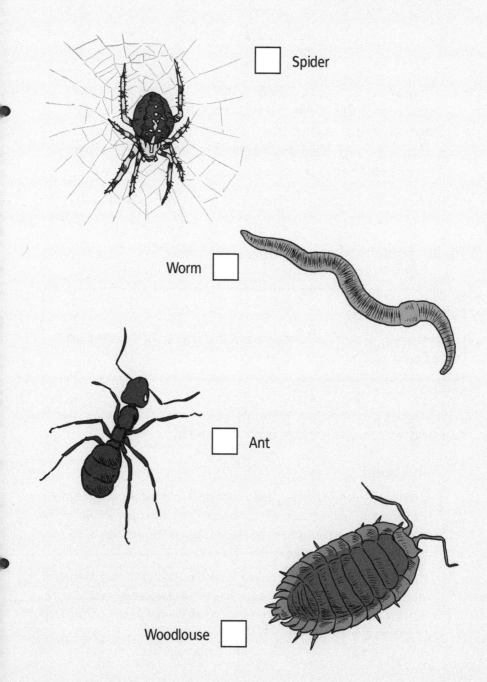

Spider

Worm

Ant

Woodlouse

23

Most bites and stings cause minor irritation. For more information about how to treat them, and information about what to do if a trooper has a more severe reaction, please see the NHS Choices page on Bites and Stings: http://www.nhs.uk/conditions/Bites-insect/Pages/Introduction.aspx, *or use your region-specific online resource*

Make your garden mini-beast friendly

⚠ **WARNING**

Please ensure all ponds are covered over with safety netting if small troopers are around.

If your troopers loved looking at mini-beasts out in the woods, you might want to take some simple steps to attract more into your garden:

- **Provide shelter**
  - If you have green fingers, you and your troopers can use plants that provide shelter—and food—to attract mini-beasts. Fruit trees are a favorite for mammals, birds and insects, while fragrant flowers like lavender, dandelions or bluebells will attract butterflies and bees
  - If you don't have green fingers, a pile of wood or rocks will attract a variety of insects such as woodlice, spiders and beetles, and require no maintenance, as will a part of your garden allowed to "go wild"—it will soon be colonized by grasses and wild flowers

- A compost bin will enable you to provide shelter for worms while also reducing waste

- **Provide food.** Find out what you want to attract to your garden, and what it feeds on. For example:

  - You can buy a variety of food for birds, but in my experience mealworm can turn any garden into a feeding frenzy

  - Bats eat moths, which can be attracted into your garden by strong-scented flowers

  - Do not leave milk out for hedgehogs; it makes them sick—use plain water instead

- **Provide water**

  - A pond, a water butt or a bowl of water are all useful sources of water

If you would like to build a bug hotel, where all kinds of mini-beasts can check in, see activity 3.6 for instructions on how to make one.

MISSION ACCOMPLISHED

I verify that on this date .... I hunted mini-beasts with my Commando Dad.

Signed:

CLIMB A TREE

Mission brief

- **Ground:** dry trees (wet bark is too slippery)
- **Situation**: a tree with a broad trunk and strong branches that your trooper can reach from the ground
- **Mission**: to conquer a tree
- **Skills:** coordination, self-esteem, risk assessment, listening and understanding

MISSION KEY

$ $ $ $ $ AGES 4+

KIT LIST:

- Trainers or flexible boots
- Basic first-aid kit

Set expectations. Climbing trees is a wonderful experience and will help your troopers appreciate nature and the great outdoors. However, failure while climbing a tree is also important. Careful trial and error is the best teacher. Encourage your trooper to dust themselves off and keep going. Victory will be so much sweeter!

INSTRUCTIONS:

Your troopers can:

1 **Select a tree.** Trees are nature's climbing frames and come in all shapes and sizes. If your troopers are new to climbing trees, go for trees that have low, thick branches and perhaps gnarly roots for them to get a good foothold. It's OK to start with a big tree as your troopers can stay in the low branches until they gain confidence.

2 **Select a route.** Encourage troopers to try to work out their route before they start to climb as this will help them to learn how to read a tree from the start. If they are happy to swing on the lower branches, this will not only help to build their confidence but also test the strength of the branches before climbing them. For the first few climbs, stay at the bottom of the tree as the troopers are more than likely to need advice about where to put their hands and feet to get up—and down—the tree.

3 **Climb.** Technique will come with time. In the beginning, troopers will scramble up the tree in the best way they can, and this should be encouraged. The object of the exercise is to climb a tree, not be concerned about how they appear to others.

Tree climbing is addictive. If you and the troopers see a great climbing tree, make a mental note of its location and head back there when circumstances permit.

MISSION ACCOMPLISHED

I verify that on this date .... I climbed to new heights with my Commando Dad.

Signed:

SCAVENGER HUNT (TWO WAYS)

Mission brief

- **Ground:** woods or forest
- **Situation:** any—you can adjust the hunt to match the season
- **Mission:** to identify key objects and experiences in the environment
- **Skills:** recognition, target acquisition, problem solving

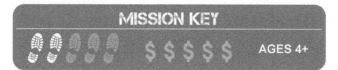

MISSION KEY

$ $ $ $ $ AGES 4+

KIT LIST:

- A scavenger hunting list (make your own, or use the spot-it sheet on page 33)

- Plastic punched pocket (one per player), which will make the list weatherproof and serve as a place to keep items

- Pencils (one per player), as they will work in all weathers and temperatures

- Antibacterial hand gel, just in case

INSTRUCTIONS:

1 **Make a scavenger list**: depending on the activity, this could be a list of items or pictures of things or sounds that you know can be found in the scavenger area, given the time of year and the terrain. Make sure your list includes a mixture of activities, as this is more engaging than just having to find things. For example:

2 **Items to find and keep**: these need to be put in their plastic pocket, so make sure they're light, small enough to carry and pretty tough. These should <u>never</u> have to be picked from the tree or plant; they should be items you can readily find on the forest floor:

- Acorns
- Pine cones
- A pine needle
- Specific leaves (make sure you provide a drawing if they're not familiar with the shape—see page 56 for some examples)

3 **Items to find and record**: these items your troopers can sketch, on the same paper as their list. Again, you'll need to have done your research if you include tracks:

- Deer tracks
- Rabbit tracks or poop (a favorite)
- Badger tracks
- Fox tracks
- Rough bark (they can make a rubbing of this; see also activity 2.1)

4 **Items to experience**: these really encourage the troopers to pay attention to what is going on in the environment around them. I don't record these; we just experience them together. But it is possible to record sounds or take pictures on your phone, if you wanted a more permanent memento:

- Listen to the wind high in the trees

- Listen to bird song
- Smell wild garlic
- Feel the bark on three different trees
- Crunch through fallen leaves

Make sure your troopers are given a trooper boundary brief, and know beforehand not to eat any berries or fungi they may find on their scavenger hunt. If you know about foraging and want to include it in your scavenger hunt, please make sure you check with the landowner beforehand, as it may not be permitted. For more information on foraging, see activity 2.15.

WAY 1—SCAVENGER HUNTING LIST:

1. **Mark the boundaries** of the hunt and ensure the troopers know them.

2. **Determine the "rally point"**—this is the location where the scavenger hunt will begin and end.

3. **Give every trooper a boundary brief,** so they understand what is safe to handle, and what is not.

4. **Give them their scavenger list.**

5. **Deploy the scavengers!**

6. **Call back the scavengers;** use the "One-Two-Three . . . Back To Me!" method.

WAY 2—PHOTOGRAPHIC MEMORY HUNT:

For older troopers who will have the ability to memorize items on a scavenger list, you can introduce a photographic memory hunt. This activity can be done individually or in pairs.

1 **Mark the boundaries of the hunt** and ensure the troopers know them.

2 **Determine the "rally point"**—this is the location where the scavenger hunt will begin and end.

3 **Give every trooper a boundary brief,** so they understand what is safe to handle, and what is not.

4 **Give each scavenger a card and, on command, they turn them over and are given time to scan and absorb the list of items.** 30 seconds to a minute is a good starting point (you can adjust it later if it was too long or short a time).

5 **Collect the card** when the memorizing time is up.

6 **Deploy the scavengers.**

7 **Call back the scavengers**; use the "One-Two-Three... Back to Me!" method.

8 **Check the scavengers' quarry to determine the winner.** Remember to be encouraging and heap lots of praise on your scavengers.

MISSION ACCOMPLISHED

I verify that on this date .... I completed a scavenger hunt with my Commando Dad.

Signed:

SCAVENGER HUNT "SPOT IT" SHEET

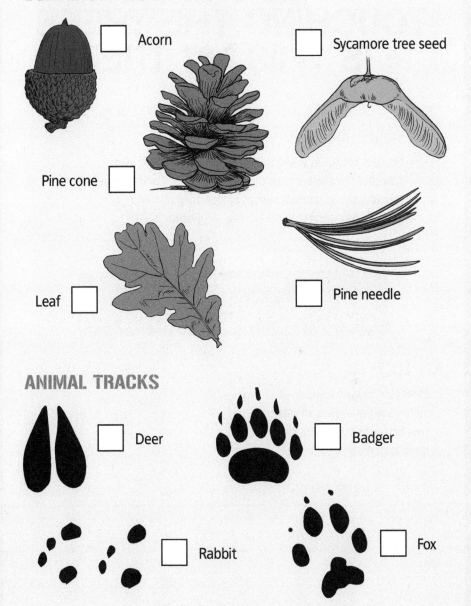

Acorn ☐

Sycamore tree seed ☐

Pine cone ☐

Leaf ☐

Pine needle ☐

ANIMAL TRACKS

Deer ☐

Badger ☐

Rabbit ☐

Fox ☐

TOUCHING THE TREES – IS THIS MY TREE?

Mission brief

- **Ground**: broadleaf woodland with a variety of tree species
- **Situation:** to explore trees through touch, smell and hearing
- **Mission:** to use multiple senses to identify your tree
- **Skills**: focus, using the senses, tree recognition

MISSION KEY

$ $ $ $ $ AGES 3+

KIT LIST:

- Blindfolds for each trooper—a cotton scarf or a spare sling from your first-aid kit would be ideal—make sure it's spare though!

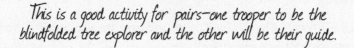

This is a good activity for pairs—one trooper to be the blindfolded tree explorer and the other will be their guide.

INSTRUCTIONS:

1. Put troopers into pairs.

2. Determine the rally point.

3. **Brief the guide to be kind to the explorer**—they will be swapping over at some point.

4. **The guide will need to choose a suitable tree.**

5. **The guide leads their partner through the forest slowly and steadily,** helping them to avoid obstacles along the way. Brief the guide to take a wiggly route to make finding the tree more difficult.

6. Once at the chosen tree, **the guide places the explorer's hands on the trunk** so they can start exploring it.

7. **The guide can help the explorer by asking questions** such as: "Does it seem big or small?," "Does it smell of anything?," "Does the bark feel smooth, rough or bumpy?"

8. **Let the explorer decide when they have finished** and the guide can lead them back to the start point, again via a wiggly route.

9. **When back at the start point, the explorer can remove their blindfold** and go off to find their tree.

10 If troopers are struggling to locate their tree, the guide can use the "hotter!" and "colder!" method of target acquisition

11 **Once the tree has been found by the explorer,** the two troopers come back to the rally point, and swap roles.

MISSION ACCOMPLISHED

I verify that on this date .... I used my senses to identify a tree with my Commando Dad.

Signed:

CAMO HAND

Mission brief

- **Ground**: in the local woods or forest
- **Situation:** to keep safe in the woods, or to hunt prey, you must be able to disappear
- **Mission:** to become a master of disguise
- **Skills**: observation, collection, camouflage

MISSION KEY

$ $ $ $ $ AGES 4+

KIT LIST:

- Collected natural materials, including a stick to stir mud
- Water to make mud (and wash it off afterwards)
- Camera to record the effectiveness of the camo if you want to review it later

In nature, camouflage is used by organisms to blend into their surroundings and avoid detection. It is used by both predator and prey animals—it allows predators to sneak up on their prey and provides a way for prey to "disappear" until the predators pass them by.

INSTRUCTIONS:

This activity has three phases, but before you begin, Commando Dad should carry out a thorough "dog-poo recce" of the area. We don't want our troopers coming across any unwanted doggie-related surprises!

1 **Close observation phase**. Have your troopers choose a tree or log, then ask them to really closely look at the different colors, textures and patterns in the wood, etc. Once they've done that, it's time to get collecting things they can find on the forest floor to help their hand become completely disguised against their chosen background. Useful materials include pieces of bark, moss, leaves, twigs, etc.

2 **Camouflage phase**. Using some of the water, earth and a stick, ask the troopers to make some mud. Using the natural materials collected, they then decorate their hand to match their selected tree or log. More ambitious troopers might decide to move higher up their arm with the camo. For younger troopers, you might decide they just have to create a camo finger.

3 **Memory phase**. If you can, take a picture of the camo hand, so later on you can reflect on how well you blended into your surroundings.

MISSION ACCOMPLISHED

I verify that on this date .... I made my camo hand disappear with my Commando Dad.

Signed:

SPOTTING STATION

Mission brief:

- **Ground**: a specific area of woods or forest
- **Situation:** there are foreign objects nearby
- **Mission:** use our powers of sight to spot and reclaim as many objects as possible
- **Skills**: observation, sense of sight, concentration

MISSION KEY

$ $ $ $ $ AGES 5+

KIT LIST:

- Ten to 15 objects of various sizes, shapes and colors—placed by you beforehand. They must be foreign to the environment—so not natural objects. Anything will do: a ball, an old toothbrush, a bicycle pump, a watering can, a plant pot... Bring some brightly colored objects that will be easier to spot, as well as objects that can blend in to the background more easily

- A bag or box to transport the objects to and from the observation area

- Paper and pencil, so that troopers can record the foreign objects they saw

- Length of string or cord

INSTRUCTIONS:

1 **Use the string to mark out a straight line.** This will be the line your spotters stand behind and also marks the limit of the Observation Area—so no objects will be placed to the left or the right of the string, only straight ahead.

2 **Place the items within the chosen area,** trying to make them difficult to spot, but not impossible. Only put objects about 20 large paces from the string, and use the whole area; put some close, some in the middle ground and some in the far ground, set at different levels. Try to match up the colors and shapes of the objects with their surroundings, so that they blend in.

3 **Before calling over the spotters,** stand behind the string and make sure you can see all of the items from various locations along its length.

4 **Bring your spotters together to stand behind the string,** and explain the activity.

5 **Ask spotters to remain quiet while observing,** and to try not to alert other spotters when they find an object.

6 **After the allotted time is up, test the spotters to see how many objects they have found.** They will have recorded the objects and they can tell you where they are located.

7 **Get the troopers to help you tidy up** at the end of the game by going and fetching the objects. It is important to make sure that every single foreign object returns home with you.

MISSION ACCOMPLISHED

I verify that on this date .... I used my powers of observation with my Commando Dad.

Signed:

STARGAZING

Mission brief

- **Ground**: open space; if camping out, a clearing in the trees
- **Situation**: a clear night, in a location with as little light pollution as possible
- **Mission**: to use the stars to find true North and tell stories from Greek mythology
- **Skills**: observation, storytelling, patience

MISSION KEY

$ $ $ $ $ AGES 3+

KIT LIST:

- Warm clothes—a clear night is a cold night as there is no cloud cover

- A red head-torch will help if your trooper is nervous in the dark (it won't impede your night vision)

INSTRUCTIONS:

1 **Find the Plough.** This constellation is made of seven stars and as long as you have a clear night, should be quite easy to identify.

2 **Locate the last two stars that make up the blade section.** Then, follow them upwards in a straight line, four times the distance between those two stars. There you will find Polaris, or the North Star. This star sits directly over the North Pole.

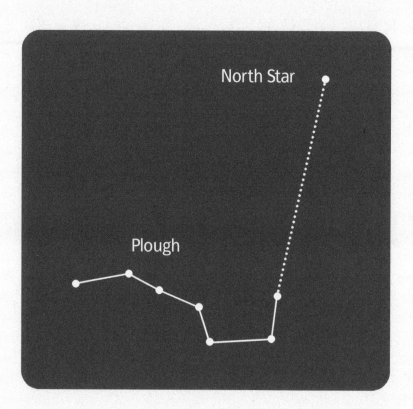

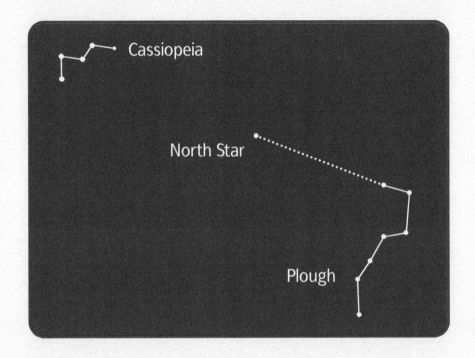

3 **If you can't find the Plough—as it may be obscured or too low in the sky—look for Cassiopeia.** It is always on the opposite side of the North Star from the Plough.

The Plough actually forms part of the constellation Ursa Major (the Great Bear). Polaris is at the end of the tail of Ursa Minor (or Little Bear). In the south you'll see Orion's Belt and the brightest star in the night sky, Sirius.

Before you set out on your stargazing adventures, find out more about the Greek myths that inspired their names. For example, Cassiopeia was a queen who boasted about her unrivalled beauty. Ursa Major wasn't always a bear—she used to be a woman named Callisto but after Zeus fell in love with her, his wife, Hera, turned her into a bear and hung her in the sky. Orion was a handsome, giant hunter and opposite him in the sky is Scorpius the Scorpion, who stung him to death.

If you and your trooper enjoyed star spotting, you can find some great resources, including a star-spotting guide, on the Jodrell Bank Discovery Center website: https://www.jodrellbank.net/learn/schools/resources/.

MISSION ACCOMPLISHED

I verify that on this date .... I gazed at the stars with my Commando Dad.

Signed:

NIGHT VISION

Mission brief:

- **Ground**: night time in the woods or forest
- **Situation**: sitting in total darkness around a crackling fire with your troopers
- **Mission**: to see in the dark like nocturnal woodland creature
- **Skills**: appreciation of how amazing your eyes are, patience, communication

MISSION KEY

$ $ $ $ AGES 4+

KIT LIST:

- A crackling campfire
- Warm clothes—when the troopers move away from the campfire they will really feel the chill
- Eye patches, or scarf, to completely cover up one eye of every trooper

At the end of a busy day in the woods adventuring, there's no better activity than sitting around the fire telling stories and melting marshmallows for your s'mores (you can find the recipe in activity 2.10). However, the fire can also offer an opportunity to experience night vision that nocturnal creatures rely on to avoid predators and to catch their prey.

INSTRUCTIONS:

1 **Before it gets dark, have the troopers collect supplies for the fire**—if you've never started a fire before, take a look at activity 2.9; that will talk you through what to do.

2 **Get the fire going** and make sure to have lots of wood to keep the fire crackling.

3 **Once it gets dark and the fire is burning brightly, cover one of your trooper's eyes with either an eye patch or a scarf**—your trooper should look like a pirate. With their uncovered eye, they should stare at the fire for a full 15 minutes (they can blink as normal!).

4 **Distract your troopers** from the time passing by chatting, telling stories or looking for shapes and faces in the fire. Make sure they do not look away from the fire during this period of time.

5 **When the 15 minutes is up, move your troopers away from the fire** and have them look into the darkness.

6 **Swap the eye covering**—so the eye that was covered up now sees and the one that looked into the fire is now covered up.

7 Your troopers will be amazed at how clearly they can see, especially as they are just using one eye. The effect will only last for a few minutes but it will really give them a sense of what it's like to have the night vision that nocturnal creatures need to survive in the woods.

MISSION ACCOMPLISHED

I verify that on this date .... I learned how to see in the dark with my Commando Dad.

Signed:

CAMPFIRE STORIES

Mission brief

- **Ground**: around the campfire in the woods or forest
- **Situation**: at the end of a long day of adventuring when evening entertainment is called for
- **Mission:** for the whole group to share stories with each other
- **Skills**: listening, imagination, communication

MISSION KEY

$ $ $ $ $ AGES 3+

KIT LIST:

- Troopers ready to listen, imagine and share a story
- A fire to sit around
- Somewhere comfortable to sit, such as a log
- Plenty of wood to keep your fire crackling

Campfires are fascinating for humans of all ages, and campfire stories are as old as the discovery of fire itself. Whereas once the stories may once have centerd around the day's hunt, or perhaps well-loved stories of the tribe, your stories are only limited by your imagination.

When I was in the forces, whenever my colleagues and I had time to relax, we'd sit round with a hot brew and tell each other stories of past adventures—where we were, who was with us, what we got up to. It was known as "swinging the lamp."

There is something very special about sitting around a crackling fire with your troopers and swinging the lamp. The key is for the storyteller to be descriptive and engaging and for the audience to use their imaginations to participate fully.

It takes practice to be able to tell a story to others, and it's never too early to get your troopers to start learning this skill.

INSTRUCTIONS:

1 **Before it gets dark, have the troopers collect supplies for the fire**. If you've never started a fire before, take a look at activity 2.9; this will talk you through what to do.

2 **Get the fire going** and make sure to have lots of wood to keep it crackling.

3 It can take a lot of courage for some troopers to be the center of attention and have everyone around the fire listening and looking at them. Lead by example. If there is a particular story you know your troopers will enjoy, telling it around the fire will bring a new dimension to the story—the sounds, the smells and the flickering of the flames will all help your troopers' imaginations go wild in the woods.

4 **Once your story has been told, you can ask one of the troopers if they would like to share a story.** If no one has the confidence at that time (don't worry—the more they experience this activity, the more their confidence will grow), you could start a story, and then ask each trooper, if they want to, to add the next part. They can add new characters, have existing characters do something exciting, or put a twist in the plot. The story could go anywhere.

5 **Make s'mores.** This is a lovely way to bring a storytelling session to a close. A s'more is basically a melted marshmallow squashed between two chocolate graham crackers or a cookie of some sort. You can find the recipe in activity 2.10.

MISSION ACCOMPLISHED

I verify that on this date .... I told campfire stories with my Commando Dad.

Signed:

SECTION 2:

LEARN

This section contains some essential outdoor skills that you can teach your troopers in one of the greatest learning environments available—the natural world.

Being outdoors in our natural environment is good for us. It's not only about physical health but mental well-being too. Research suggests that when we're in nature the alpha waves in our brain—which indicate a calm but alert state—grow stronger. Learning outdoors promotes curiosity and exploration, and encourages skills such as problem-solving and negotiating risk, which are important for your trooper's development. In fact, the rich, changing environment offers stimulus for all areas of development and all learning styles: visual, auditory and kinaesthetic (body awareness). It encourages troopers to learn independently and to assess their own learning and experiences. What are you waiting for?

TREE ID

Mission brief

- **Ground**: woods and forest at any time of year
- **Situation**: a rich environment with diverse tree species
- **Mission**: to identify trees using a variety of evidence
- **Skills**: tree recognition, nature appreciation, recall

MISSION KEY

$ $ $ $ $ AGES 4+

KIT LIST:

- Spotting sheets
- Plastic punched pockets to keep the sheets dry and collect small pieces of evidence if needed
- A pencil for troopers to record what they saw (or perhaps sketch something they didn't recognize so they can research it later)

Identifying trees by their leaves, twigs and fruit is a great skill for your troopers to develop as they spend time in the woods. Knowing, and being able to recognize trees, is an important step in helping your troopers begin to feel more at home in the outdoors environment. This activity requires a thorough reconnaissance mission (or recce) of the woods by Commando Dad, so you know what species of trees your troopers will find when you arrive.

MAKING A SPOTTING SHEET:

Your spotting sheets need to include as many clues as possible to help your troopers identify different trees. Depending on the time of year, you could include:

- Leaves
- Twigs
- Blossom
- Fruit, nuts and seeds

Spotting sheets cover all seasons so will spark some great conversations that will help educate troopers about the life of trees throughout the year, such as:

- Why do some trees have leaves that fall off?
- Why don't trees have flowers all year?
- Why do trees have different fruits?

To get you started, here are five leaves from trees you might find in your local woods.

Oak

Horse chestnut

Sycamore

Hazel

Rowan

INSTRUCTIONS:

1 Determine the rally point.

2 Give each trooper a spotting sheet and explain the rules.

3 **Explore together** to piece together clues to identify trees.

4 **Test your trooper's understanding** by asking them to identify trees, leaves, twigs and so on at other visits to woodland.

5 If your trooper would like to, they can start to build a tree ID scrapbook at home. They can use fallen leaves or seeds they find in this activity or on a scavenger hunt (activity 1.4), any sketches they make when out in the woods, leaf prints (activity 3.4) and rubbings of tree bark (activity 3.5)

MISSION ACCOMPLISHED

I verify that on this date .... I learned how to ID a tree with my Commando Dad.

Signed:

MAKE A TEMPLATE FOR TYING KNOTS

Mission brief

- **Ground**: base camp
- **Situation**: any
- **Mission**: to create a portable knot-tying template to enable troopers to practise and perfect four important knots: overhand knot, figure-of-eight knot, reef knot and bowline.
- **Skills**: dexterity, construction, tool use

MISSION KEY

$ $ $ $ $ AGES 4+

KIT LIST:

- Stiff cardboard 28 x 21 cm (11 x 8 in.) approx.
- 2.5 m (8 ft) of cord in a single color
- Scissors
- Pencil
- Ruler
- Marker pen
- Phillips-head screwdriver

WARNING

These instructions include using a screwdriver for making holes in stiff cardboard, and this activity should only be undertaken by a Commando Dad. It also involves cutting cord with scissors so please exercise caution, common sense and close supervision if you intend to let your trooper undertake this task

INSTRUCTIONS:

1 **Measure twice and cut once.** On the back of the card:

- Draw three straight lines at 7-cm (3-in.) intervals, using your pencil and ruler.
- Draw two horizontal lines at 7-cm (3 in). intervals.

2 You now have 12 boxes.

- The first row is for labels.
- The second row is for the knots, tied correctly as an example.
- The third row is for the practice cord.

3 In the first three boxes on the second and third rows, **mark out a hole in the dead center**.

4 In the final box on the second and third row **mark out two holes in the center** of the box, about 3 cm (1 in.) apart.

5 When you have the marks in the right place, go over the pencil mark with the marker.

6 **Create the holes.** Place the cardboard on a flat surface and use the Phillips-head screwdriver to push and twist through. Lift it to finish off so that you can push the screwdriver all the way through. Repeat on the other side of the card, for all ten holes. Label your template so it looks like this:

Overhand knot	Figure-of-eight knot	Bowline	Reef/square knot
◯	◯	◯	◯ ◯
◯	◯	◯	◯ ◯

7 **Create the knots.** Cut the cord onto eight roughly equal lengths. Thread a length through the holes, securing at the back with a stopper knot, apart from the last box where the lengths of cord fall at the front of the template.

8 On the middle row, tie the following knots correctly (see activity 2.3):

- The overhand knot—single hole.
- The figure-of-eight knot—single hole.
- The bowline—single hole.
- The reef knot—two holes.

9 Your knot tying template is now ready to be deployed.

For a more permanent template solution, you could use a thin board and a drill, but I find the method described here makes for a more collaborative activity.

MISSION ACCOMPLISHED

I verify that on this date .... I began to learn that practice makes perfect with my Commando Dad.

Signed:

KNOT TYING

Mission brief

- **Ground**: anywhere
- **Situation**: when a knot is required to fasten something
- **Mission**: to learn how to use four important knots
- **Skills**: hand–eye coordination, dexterity, strength of hand muscles

MISSION KEY

$ $ $ $ $ AGES 4+

KIT LIST:

- Several lengths of cord or thin rope

NOTES:

Four very useful knots for your troopers to learn are:

- The overhand or thumb knot
- The figure-of-eight knot
- The square or reef knot
- The bowline

The first step is to understand the anatomy of the rope:

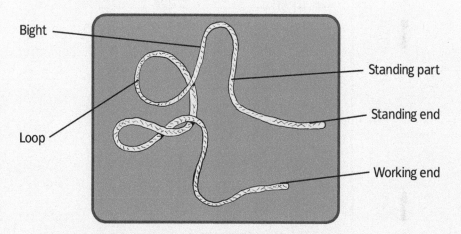

- **Working end:** the end of the rope you're using to tie a knot.
- **Standing end:** the opposite end to the working end.
- **Standing part:** any part between the two ends. It can be part of the rope already used in the knot.
- **Loop:** a loop made by turning the rope back on itself and crossing the standing part.
- **Bight:** a loop made by turning the rope back on itself without crossing the standing part.

OVERHAND OR THUMB KNOT:

This simple knot (which is tied in the end of a line) is quick and easy to tie, and is often used as a stopper at the end of a rope. It is the perfect first knot to learn as it forms the basis of more complicated knots.

INSTRUCTIONS:

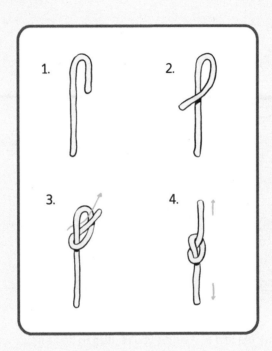

1. **Form an overhand loop,** by taking the working end in a clockwise direction over the standing end

2. **Make a single overhand knot** by passing the working end into the loop from below. Pull through sufficient line at the working end to finish the knot.

The figure-of-eight knot:

The figure-of-eight knot is one of the strongest stopper knots, and forms a secure and non-slip loop at the end of a rope. It is often used by mountain climbers, not only because it is so strong but also because it is easy to inspect.

A rhyme to help you remember how to tie this knot: "Twist it once, twist it twice; pass it through and make it nice."

INSTRUCTIONS:

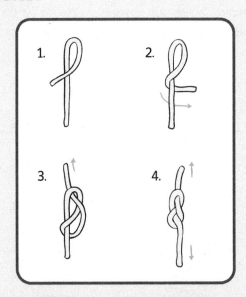

1. Twist it once: make an overhand loop with the working end, twisting anticlockwise.

2 **Twist it twice:** twist the loop again anticlockwise.

3 **Pass it through:** pass the working end up into the loop to complete the knot.

4 **Make it nice:** tidy up by pulling on either end of your knot.

The square or reef knot:

This knot is used to tie together two working ends of the same material and size, to secure something that is not likely to move about. It lies flat when tied with cloth, making it particularly useful for bandages.

A mnemonic to help you remember how to tie this knot: "Left over right and under, then right over left and under."

INSTRUCTIONS:

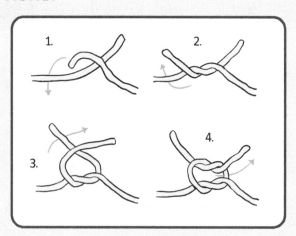

1. **Put the left hand working end** over the right.

2. **Twist the upper working end** around, under and back to the front.

3. **Bend the working ends towards each other**, right going over left.

4. **Twist the upper working end** around, under and back to the front.

5. **Tidy up** by pulling on each working end.

The bowline:

The bowline is used to make a loop at one end of a rope or line. It forms a secure loop that is easy to tie and untie, making it one of the most useful knots. It can be used for tasks such as a rope swing seat, and in the construction of a tarp shelter.

A rhyme to help you remember how to tie this knot: "Up through the rabbit hole, round the big tree; down through the rabbit hole and off goes he."

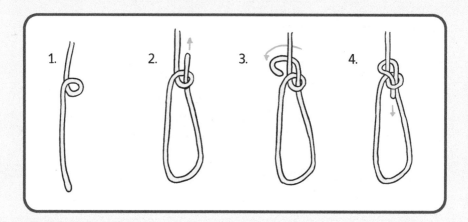

INSTRUCTIONS:

1 **Create the "rabbit hole"** by crossing the working end over the rope to form a "b" shape.

2 **Up through the hole:** bring the free end up through the loop you created.

3 **Round the big tree:** bring the free end around the back of the working end.

4 **Down the rabbit hole and off goes he:** then place it back down through the loop and tighten.

MISSION ACCOMPLISHED

I verify that on this date .... I started to learn how to tie knots with my Commando Dad.

Signed:

BUILD A FAIRY VILLAGE

Mission brief

- **Ground:** woods, forest or local park
- **Situation:** a sneezing dragon has swept away fairy homes
- **Mission:** to build new fairy dens
- **Skills:** imagination, cooperation, construction

MISSION KEY

$ $ $ $ $ AGES 3+

KIT LIST:

- Natural materials, such as leaves, moss, stones and twigs

INSTRUCTIONS:

1 **Set the scene** by telling a story to explain why fairies need your troopers' help to rebuild their village. I've put a story below—but feel free to make up your own.

Do you troopers believe in fairies? No? Well, that's because people moved out of woods so long ago that we have got used to not seeing them. In turn, fairies have grown frightened of humans and so they hide away when they hear us. Chances are they are very nearby right now, because on the very spot on which you're standing, there used to be the most amazing fairy village. It had houses with lovely gardens, little shops, a school and a place where the fairies could dance.

So where is it now?

The fairy folk in this wood are very friendly, and one of their best friends is a lovely dragon who lives over the other side of the wood. He loves to dance, just like the fairies, and so they invited him to their annual fairy dance last night. As he put on his dancing shoes, he felt a little tickle in his nose. The dragon realized that he'd caught a cold but he was so excited about the dance, he thought "I'll just go for a little boogie, then come straight home to bed!"

By the time he reached the village, he was sneezing away, and every time he sneezed, because of his powerful breath, he knocked down fairy buildings in the village! By the time his sneezing had stopped, the whole village had been flattened, so the poor fairies had no choice but to move to a new, secret location. It's a really sad story, but do you think we might be able to help the fairy folk?

1. After the story, help the troopers decide what they would like to have in their new fairy village.

2. **Have them explore the area** to look for interesting areas and characteristics that could be used in the new village—a hole at the base of a tree, twisting roots, low hanging branches, etc.

3. **Explain to your troopers that fairies really like things to look pretty** and then ask them to collect fairy den-building materials from the forest floor—with a view to keeping fairies safe, warm and dry in an amazing-looking fairy den.

4. **Let construction commence.** When your troopers are happy that they have made the best fairy village they can, it's time to leave so that the fairies can come and move into their new homes.

MISSION ACCOMPLISHED

I verify that on this date .... I helped the fairies find a new home with my Commando Dad.

Signed:

BUILD A NATURAL SHELTER

Mission brief

- **Ground:** woods, best around autumn time so you have plenty of leaves. Check with the landowner that you can build a shelter (and perhaps even sleep out in it)
- **Situation:** calm weather, especially if you intend to sleep out in it
- **Mission:** to create a natural shelter
- **Skills:** teamwork, communication, self-reliance

MISSION KEY

$ $ $ $ $ AGES 5+

KIT LIST:

- Ridge pole: a straight long branch as thick as your forearm. It determines the length of the shelter so needs to be longer than the tallest person in the shelter. It needs to be alive— that is, green, and have sap in it—to be strong enough to use

- Two sturdy trees to rest the ridge pole against. They should be just over the body length

of the tallest person apart.

- Two strong forked sticks to hold up the ridge pole, as tall as the chest of the tallest person. Again, these need to be alive.

- Brash (foliage on the woodland floor), longer branches to create the roof, and lots of twigs and branches.

WARNING:

You might need to use a saw or a knife to complete this mission. In addition to exercising extreme caution around the troops, please see Knives and the Law on pages 204–205 to ensure that you understand the law and that you are adhering to it.

INSTRUCTIONS:

Before you start building your shelter, you need to select the right site. So, consider the following:

- **Materials:** for this shelter, choose an area where there are plenty of sticks, branches for poles, leaves and ferns.
- **Comfort:** check the floor for roots and rocks before you start building. Keep away from insect nests. Check to make sure the ground is not wet or liable to flood if it rains heavily.
- **Safety:** look all around for hazards before you start building, including falling trees and pooling water.

1 When you have chosen the best site, place the two forked sticks on the inside of your selected trees.

2 Place the ridge pole between the forks of your sticks, making sure the pole goes BEHIND your selected trees, and protrudes at least 30 cm (12 in.) at each end.

3 Adjust the angle of the forked sticks so that they lean about 45 degrees, and make sure the end of your forked stick is embedded 18–20 cm (7–8 in.) into the ground so that it won't slip. This angle also helps secure your ridge pole in place, and stops any lateral movement.

4️⃣ Test the strength of your ridge pole by hanging off its center. It should hold your weight. If it does, continue. If not, find another ridge pole.

5️⃣ The 45-degree angle you've created with your forked sticks gives you the slope of your "roof," and you're now ready to start creating your waterproof covering.

6️⃣ Lean longer sticks and branches against the ridge pole, at about every 30 cm (12 in.). They must extend about 20–30 cm (8–12 in.) above the ridge pole. These will act as roof supports.

7️⃣ Arrange branches, brash and twigs on top of the roof supports, until the canopy is thick and sturdy. Aim for a depth between fist and elbow deep to ensure it is insulated and waterproof.

8️⃣ Starting from the bottom, begin laying dead leaves all over the shelter.

9 When you think the outside of the shelter is complete, go and lie in it. If you see any daylight, add more leaves.

10 Prepare your floor with a thick mattress of brash. This is essential to insulate the troopers from the cold ground.

The aim is to make the shelter just big enough to accommodate your unit. Making the shelter any larger is a waste of time, resources and energy, and any unused extra space on the inside will also make your shelter colder than it would be if it were a little more snug.

MISSION ACCOMPLISHED

I verify that on this date .... I sheltered with my Commando Dad.

Signed:

BUILD A TARP SHELTER

Mission brief
- **Ground:** woods—check with the landowner that it's OK to build a shelter (and perhaps even sleep out in it)
- **Situation:** calm weather, especially if you intend to sleep out in it
- **Mission:** to create a tarp shelter
- **Skills:** teamwork, communication, self-reliance, knot tying

MISSION KEY

$ $ $ $ $ AGES 6+

KIT LIST:

- Tarpaulin (tarp) with grommets (these are reinforced holes that allow you to put up your shelter). Choose the one that's the right size for your group

- Paracord, string or twine to attach the tarp to trees. Six to eight lengths, 1 m (3 ft) each, will do the job. It is always better to have longer lengths as you can tie them off to make them the required length

- Three stakes to attach your shelter to the ground. These need to be about 15 cm (6 in.) long and 3 cm (1 in.) wide, so look for suitable sticks or you can use normal tent pegs

- Mallet, if you have one, to drive your stakes/tent pegs down. If not, just improvise and use a rock (a task for Commando Dad)

- Two trees, to anchor the shelter, about 3–5 m (10–15 ft) apart

- Brash (foliage on the woodland floor) and lots of twigs and branches

INSTRUCTIONS:

Before you begin:

- To secure your tarp shelter, you'll need to know three "hitch" knots:
  - For the fixed end of your ridgeline, you can use a **Siberian hitch.**
  - To tighten the ridgeline, you can use a **trucker's hitch**. This will provide tension to your tarp.
  - For the corners of your tarp, you need an adjustable knot, so you can use a **tautline hitch.**

Siberian hitch:

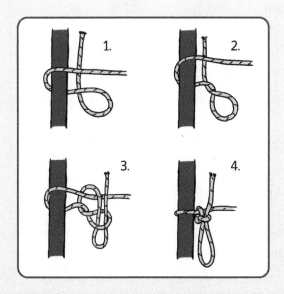

- Swing your rope/cord around the tree, then put the working end under the cord where the load is going to be, i.e. under your ridgeline.
- Make a loop in the free end, making sure that the ends going around the tree are parallel (see step 1 in the diagram).
- Twist your loop once (see step 2).

- Make a bight in the working end, bring it over the standing part (ridgeline), then feed it through your loop and tighten.

To release, simply pull on the working end and the knot will untie.

Trucker's hitch:

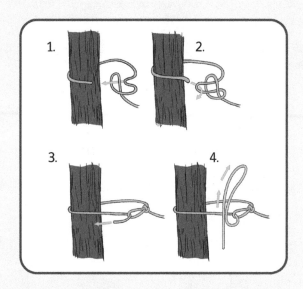

- Swing your rope/cord around your tree, make a loop and hold.

- Bring the standing part towards the tree in a bight, then push it through the loop you've just created. (See step 1 in diagram). Pull the standing part and standing end to pinch the bight and make a loop on your line.

- Feed the working end through the loop you've just created, creating a pulley system. Pull the working end towards the tree to create tension in your ridgeline (see step 3). Make sure you have at least 20 cm (8 in.) of rope at your working end.

- Once you're happy with the tension in the ridgeline, hold the working end firm. Make a large bight in the working end and drape it over the standing part leading from your loop in the line to the tree (see step 4).

- Take your working end, make a bight, and pass it under and through the draped bight. Capture the second bight by tightening the line around it. This leaves you with a quick-release option—just pull the working end to release the hitch.

Tautline hitch:

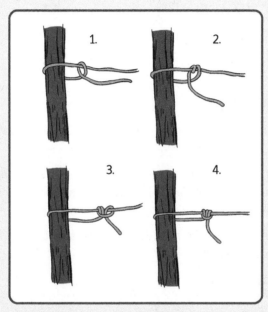

- This is an adjustable knot. One end of the rope will be attached to the tarp, using a round turn and two half hitches.

- Swing your rope/cord around your tree, and put the working end over the cord that is heading towards your tarp.

- Wrap the working end three times around the tarp cord, then bring the cord parallel to the tarp cord.

- Go below and wrap around and through. You can now adjust the knot up and down to adjust tension.

INSTRUCTIONS:

Improvisation is the name of the game with tarp shelters. These instructions are for a canopy-type shelter, but you can also make a more traditional A-frame shelter and any number of combinations.

1 **Before you start** building your shelter, you need to select the right site. So consider the following:

- **Materials:** for this shelter, choose an area with two trees about 3–5 m (10–16 ft) apart.

- **Comfort:** check the floor for roots and rocks before you start building. These can be really uncomfortable to lie on. Keep away from insect nests. Check to make sure the ground is not wet or liable to flood if it rains heavily.

- **Safety:** look all around for hazards before you start building, including falling trees and pooling water.

Pitching instructions:

2 Make the ridgeline or tension your tarp:

- Take two small sticks to help secure your tarp cords to the grommets at either corner of your tarp. This will make sure that pressure is distributed evenly and prevent the grommets from being torn out. You can also use a round turn and two half hitches to attach your tarp cords to the grommets.

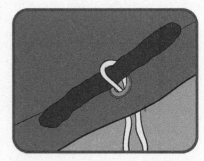

3 Using the Siberian hitch, attach one end of the tarp to the first tree, at about shoulder height.

4 Using the trucker's hitch, attach the opposite end of the tarp to the opposite tree and tighten. The tighter the tension of your ridgeline or tarp, the stronger your shelter will be.

5 When that's secure, attach tarp cords to the loose corner grommets and edge grommets of the tarp, using a tautline hitch, and then stake the shelter to the ground.

6 Climb under your shelter.

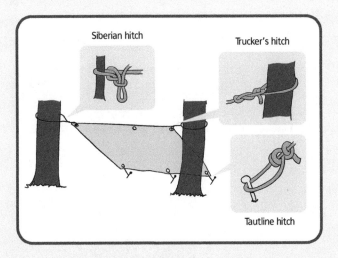

MISSION ACCOMPLISHED

I verify that on this date .... I created a tarp shelter, secured with knots and lashings, with my Commando Dad.

Signed:

READ A COMPASS

Mission brief

- **Ground**: any
- **Situation**: any
- **Mission**: to learn the basics of compass reading and work out the direction of travel
- **Skills**: confidence, self-esteem, communication

MISSION KEY

$ $ $ $ $ AGES 5+

KIT LIST:

- A compass

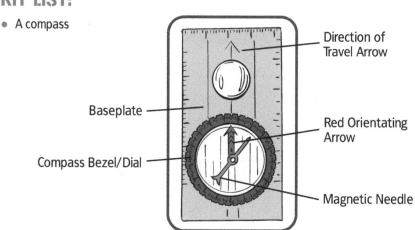

Direction of Travel Arrow

Baseplate

Red Orientating Arrow

Compass Bezel/Dial

Magnetic Needle

INSTRUCTIONS:

Before they learn to read the compass, troopers must understand its basic layout. The principle is that the compass has a magnetized needle that orients itself to the Earth's magnetic field and always points to magnetic north.

Your trooper should:

1 **Hold the compass correctly:** in the outstretched palm of the hand, at chest level.

2 **Work out the direction they're facing** by looking at the magnetic needle (the only part of the compass that moves independently). The bezel can also be moved by the trooper navigating.

- If the trooper is facing north, everything will line up with the red orientating arrow.

- If the trooper is not facing north, the magnetic needle will be moving to the left or right of the orientating arrow. **The magnetic needle always faces magnetic north.**

- The trooper should adjust the bezel of the compass (not their position) until the orientating arrow lines up with the magnetic needle.

- The "direction of travel" arrow on the compass will indicate the direction your trooper is facing. It may be between two compass points:
  - North and east: northeast.
  - South and east: southeast.

- South and west: southwest.
- North and west: northwest.

3 More accurate information can be gathered by **looking at where the direction of travel arrow meets the degree dial**. So, for example, if it intersects at 60, the trooper is facing 60 degrees in that direction (for example, 60 degrees northwest).

4 **Encourage your trooper** to move to different places and work out their position, until they are comfortable with reading the compass and its basic layout.

MISSION ACCOMPLISHED

I verify that on this date .... I started to learn compass reading, as a foundation for future explorations with my Commando Dad.

Signed:

MAKE A BOTTLE FILTER

Mission brief

- **Ground**: woods or forest with a water source
- **Situation**: to survive, we need to keep hydrated—so we need drinkable water
- **Mission**: to make a water filter using natural materials
- **Skills**: teamwork, creativity, survival skills

MISSION KEY

$ $ $ $ AGES 6+

KIT LIST:

- Scissors
- Plastic bottles
- Mess tin or pan to collect your filtered water
- Piece of cloth big enough to push down into the neck of the bottle
- You need a combination of small material and larger items so that you can create different layers in your bottle filter: ground charcoal, gravel, grass, leaves, wood shavings and pine cones

One essential requirement for survival in the wilderness is access to safe, clean water. This bottle filter will remove particles of dirt and debris, but not the bacteria that can live in water. For that, we need to boil water. The combination of filtering and boiling water makes it safe for us to drink and use for cooking.

INSTRUCTIONS:

1 Have your troopers **gather up the materials** they'll need for their bottle filter.

2 To make the bottle filter:

- Cut the bottom off the plastic bottle and remove the lid.
- Wedge the piece of cloth into the neck of the bottle.

- Fill the bottle with layers in this particular order—making sure they are tightly compacted:

  ○ Ground charcoal.

  ○ Gravel.

  ○ Grass and leaves.

  ○ Wood shavings.

  ○ Pine cones.

3 Your layers must be in this order. The larger particles will be filtered out by the pine cones and wood shavings; the water will be cleaned and the smaller debris removed by the crushed charcoal and cloth.

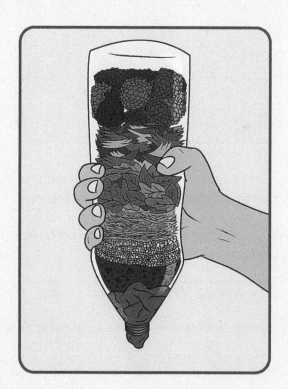

4 **Pour your muddy water into the top of your filter**—slowly and steadily. Take care not to spill the water over the sides as it will contaminate your clean water.

5 **Pour the water through your filter several times**—each time it goes through the layers, more debris is removed and the water is cleaner.

6 If you want to use this water for drinking, you need to **heat it to a rolling boil** to kill off any potentially harmful bacteria.

MISSION ACCOMPLISHED

I verify that on this date .... I made dirty water safe to drink with my Commando Dad.

Signed:

BUILD A FIRE

Mission brief

- **Ground:** woodland—check with the landowner if they allow fires on their land
- **Situation:** when you and the unit need warmth and/or a method of cooking
- **Mission:** to build and light a fire
- **Skills:** managing risk, problem solving, perseverance

MISSION KEY

$ $ $ $ $ AGES 5+

KIT LIST:

- An ignition source: matches or a lighter are a great place to start, but if you want to try a more advanced method, I've included instructions for a fire steel

- Stones to build your fire circle

- A garden trowel to dig a fire pit (if not using stones)

- A protective glove for putting wood into the fire

- Tinder to catch the initial spark from the ignition source and transfer it to the kindling. If the kindling is damp or wet, the tinder must burn long enough to dry out the kindling. Good sources: dead dry plants and grasses, wood shavings, cotton wool

- Kindling, which needs more bulk than tinder so it can ignite easily, produce sustained heat and flame, and light the main fuel source. Good sources: dry twigs and wood pieces

- Bulky fuel sources for sustained burning. Good sources: dry wood that is 3–15 cm (1–6 in.) diameter, peat, dried animal dung, coal.

 WARNING

Please exercise caution, common sense and close supervision throughout every stage of this exercise and give your troopers a trooper boundary brief before you begin. It might be a good idea to practise in the garden back at base camp before venturing out and about.

INSTRUCTIONS:

1 **Have the troopers gather tinder, kindling and wood** to help make the fire. Explain the different sizes they'll need to get the fire going (see below). Make sure they get plenty of wood as fires can be very hungry.

2 **Clear a circular area about 1.2 m (4 ft) in diameter** (the "fire circle").

3 **Build a ring of rocks** to create the fire circle to insulate the fire (alternatively, dig a fire pit about 15 cm (6 in.) deep with a small garden trowel). In the center, build a small platform from dry twigs and small sticks for your fire to sit on.

Explain to the troopers why you need to take such care when building the base of the fire. Ask them to imagine sitting straight on the forest floor after a shower of rain. Their bottoms would quickly get wet and cold, and soon after they would be cold all over because the ground would draw the heat away from their body. It's the same for a fire. You have to make sure its bottom is kept warm and dry!

4 Divide the dry wood into three bundles:

- Wood as thin as a matchstick and as long as your arm (size 1)
- Wood as thin as your finger and as long as your arm (size 2)
- Wood as thick as your wrist and as long as your arm (size 3)

5 Place your tinder onto the small platform you created in the center of your fire circle and light it.

- If using matches or a lighter simply light the tinder.
- If using the fire steel, place the striker flat at the top of the fire rod and use your strength to firmly push them together. Maintaining that pressure, and with the end of the rod pinning down your tinder, tilt the striker to a 45-degree angle and scrape all the way down the rod to create your sparks. Be careful not to go too fast, as you may end up scattering your tinder far and wide.

6 **When the tinder is alight, carefully put on a bundle of size 1 sticks—**
remember that if you put too little on, the fire won't take. This kindling needs
to be dense enough to light but spaced out enough to enable air to circulate
(fire needs oxygen to burn). Once you hear a gentle crackling, the fire is
starting to take. Lay on another bundle of size 1 sticks, holding them carefully
by the ends. Lay these on in a criss-cross pattern, a bit like when setting up a
Jenga game. This allows more air to flow into the center of your fire.

7 As the fire gets hotter, you'll need to wear a protective glove when adding more
fuel.

8 **Continue laying on the wood in this criss-cross fashion,** gradually adding size
2 sticks when all the size 1s have gone before eventually moving to size 3.

9 When laying on your size 3 bundles of wood, use the best lay for the task at
hand because different lays are better for different tasks. See below for more
information on lays for warmth for a group or cooking, and online for other fire-
lay variations.

FIRE LAYS AND THEIR USES:

THE TEEPEE FIRE

This lay is good for creating heat for a group to sit around. It is not good for cooking, as it doesn't create very many embers and is not flat.

- Arrange the tinder and a few sticks of kindling in the shape of a cone.
- Stick four kindling twigs in the ground to form a teepee above the tinder.
- Leave an opening through which you can light the fire, ideally on the upwind side to ensure any flame will blow up and towards the wood.
- Build up the rest of the teepee, from small kindling twigs to larger twigs to logs, making sure there is room for air to circulate.
- Light the tinder at the center.
- As the flames become established, the outside logs will fall inward and feed the fire.

THE CRISS-CROSS OR UPSIDE-DOWN FIRE:

This lay is good for producing embers for cooking. This fire is a bit of a rule breaker, as the lay is thick at the bottom and gets progressively thinner as it moves up the fire.

- Place the biggest logs at the bottom, then criss-cross your size 3, size 2 and size 1 bundles on top.

- Place your tinder on top, and once it's lit, gravity will assist in dropping the hot embers down onto the fuel below.

- These embers will ignite each layer below, and the fire will grow.

Putting a fire out safely:

If you want to leave the site before the fire has burned out naturally, you will need to put it out and return the area to as close as possible to how you found it. Remember, a Commando Dad adopts a "leave no trace" attitude when doing any activity in the great outdoors.

- Poke the burning items away from each other.

- Soak the fire and surrounding area with water—this helps take the heat away from the ground around the fire, preventing it from spontaneously restarting.

- When there is no smoke the fire is out.

MISSION ACCOMPLISHED

I verify that on this date .... I tapped into a primal instinct—to make fire—with my Commando Dad.

Signed:

FOREST COOKING

Mission brief

- **Ground**: woods, forest or your own garden
- **Situation**: when your fire has hot embers
- **Mission**: to make food in the outdoors, where it invariably tastes better
- **Skills**: self-reliance, confidence, nutrition

MISSION KEY

$ $ $ $ $ AGES 4+

There is something very special about cooking and eating in the great outdoors, especially if that cooking is done on a campfire. To efficiently cook the recipes below, you need a fire that has plenty of hot embers. Use the Criss-Cross/Upside Down fire lay in activity 2.9.

FIRE BREAD:
Makes 4
KIT LIST:

- Bowl
- Fireproof gloves
- Four clean sticks (to wrap dough around), 1 m (3 ft) long

- 175g (6 oz.) self-raising flour
- A few splashes of water
- Butter (optional)

INSTRUCTIONS:

1 **Mix together the flour and water.** You need a dough that holds together but doesn't stick to your hands. If it's like breadcrumbs, add more water—if it's too gooey, add more flour.

2 **Divide the dough** into tennis ball sized balls and roll it into a long sausage shape.

3 **Twist the dough sausage around your fire stick.**

4 **Hold the stick over the embers** for 10–15 minutes, turning it to ensure an even cook.

5 When it is cooked, it will sound hollow when you tap it.

6 Eat as is, or with butter.

CAMPFIRE JACKET POTATOES:
Makes 4
KIT LIST:

- Kitchen foil
- Fireproof gloves
- Forks or spoons to eat with
- 4 baking potatoes, cleaned

- 4 tbsp of butter
- Fillings if required, such as butter, grated cheese, beans, coleslaw

INSTRUCTIONS:

1 **Pierce each potato** with a fork before smearing with 1 tablespoon of butter.

2 **Double-wrap each potato** in silver foil.

3 **Bury the potatoes** in the hot embers.

4 **Allow to cook** for 45–60 minutes until soft.

5 **Carefully unwrap each potato**, slice open and serve with the filling of your choice.

S'MORES:
Makes 4
KIT LIST:

- 4 wooden skewers
- Fireproof gloves
- 8 big marshmallows

- 8 chocolate graham crackers or plain graham crackers if you don't like, or can't eat, chocolate—use butterscotch chips, peanut butter or even lemon curd instead of choccy!

INSTRUCTIONS:

1 **Place a marshmallow onto the end of a wooden skewer,** making sure it is long enough so that you or your troopers can stay a safe distance from the fire.

2 **Hold over the embers,** and keep turning until the marshmallow is toasted and gooey.

3 **Blow on it** for a full 30 seconds.

4 **Place the melted marshmallow between two chocolate graham crackers,** chocolate sides touching the marshmallow.

5 Squash together and enjoy.

MISSION ACCOMPLISHED

I verify that on this date .... I cooked up a campfire storm with my Commando Dad.

Signed:

TRACK WOODLAND CREATURES

Mission brief

- **Ground:** woods and forest
- **Situation:** winter is especially useful as there is less foliage to hide tracks, etc.
- **Mission:** to track the diverse wildlife in our woodland
- **Skills:** tracking, observation, woodland animal recognition

MISSION KEY

$ $ $ $ $ AGES 4+

KIT LIST:

- A camera or smartphone if you want to record finds

- A spotting sheet of woodland wildlife. This will help to prepare the troopers beforehand and later when they are reviewing their photos/pictures. You can find great downloadable spotting sheets for UK wildlife at www.wildlifewatch.org.uk/spotting-sheets or your troopers can make their own. International readers can search online for "wildlife spotting sheet" and find results more specific to your geographic location

- Binoculars if available, as troopers love them

Set clear expectations here. Woodland creatures are elusive, practised in concealing themselves and expert at avoiding their top predator: people. This means that the unit may track the signs of them all day but not catch a glimpse.

INSTRUCTIONS:

1 **Decide how serious you want to be.** If you want to track wildlife, you'll need to be quiet, camouflaged (not cammed up, nor in very bright clothes that make it even easier to be spotted by wildlife) and probably in the woods very early in the morning, or at dusk. If this is something your troopers are interested in, then you will want to follow as many of the steps below as possible in an attempt to track—and hopefully find—the animal you're looking for. However, if your troopers don't have the patience, inclination or time to track animals, it can still be a great adventure to follow some of the steps and look for the clues below. Older troopers may also enjoy using a camera to capture what they find.

2 **Do your research** so you know what to look for, and where. Pick your day and route carefully. If you go to an area popular with dog walkers for example, you're even less likely to see any woodland animals. Make sure to add birds to your list, as even if woodland mammals prove elusive you'll normally be able to spot a bird or two.

3 **Walk into the breeze** to avoid animals catching your smell. If you have found something you want to monitor (for example, a badger sett—in which case you'd need to be there around sunset), climb a tree to lessen your scent.

4 **Be silent.** If you need to talk, whisper. You might want to agree on a code beforehand (no sudden movements though) such as:

- Index finger to lips (silence).
- Hold your fist up, palm side facing outward (stop).
- Index and middle finger of one hand to each of the eyes and then point with the same hand (look in that direction).
- Touching the top of the head with the fingers ("on me" or "come to me").

5 **Think like the animal you're tracking.** This will help you work out where you're most likely to find them. For example, the main diet of a badger is earthworms, which favor grassy fields. Woods are a good place to start looking for badger tracks and setts. Deer eat bark and so look for trees where the bark has fresh vertical marks from a recent meal.

Blue tit

6 **Look for footprints.** This is especially effective in winter because plants will have died back, which makes tracks in mud especially easy to find. Tracks also show up well in snow.

7 **Look for homes.** Many woodland animals build their homes in the ground:

- Badger sett: most likely on sloping ground, with a wide hole at the opening. Fresh piles of earth around the sett mean that it is in use.
- Rabbit warrens: most likely on slopes or banks. The holes are typically round or oval.
- Wood mice or vole holes: most likely to be under tree roots. Often camouflaged with twigs, earth and stones.
- Rat holes: most likely close to water and under a cover, such as tree roots. Likely to have freshly dug soil outside.
- Water vole holes: very similar to a rat hole in that it is close to the water's

edge (and these voles are sometimes known as water rats). They prefer steep-sided earthy banks beside slow-moving water, and their holes are roughly circular.

Water vole

8 **Look for poop.** This will help you figure out the animal's identity. If it's fresh, that means the animal was there recently. There's also some great poop-spotting sheets available online. I guarantee that's one piece of homework no trooper is ever going to complain about.

9 **Look for fur and feathers.** It can sometimes get caught on brambles or fences and will give you a clue about what animals have passed through.

Finding Wildlife:

If you are lucky enough to be rewarded with spotting wildlife:

- **Stay still:** keep the elation contained and silent or you will simply frighten them away.

- **Observe**: what are they doing? Are they young or old? Unless you are able to take a photo in absolute silence and without taking your eyes off the animal, I would recommend that you just be present for those few precious moments.

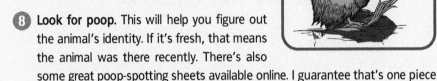

MISSION ACCOMPLISHED

I verify that on this date .... I answered the call of the wildlife with my Commando Dad.

Signed:

KNIFE SAFETY AND SKILLS

Knives are a very important tool in the great outdoors and allowing your trooper to use one is a big step that comes with a great deal of responsibility. You need to be sure that your trooper is ready for the responsibility. Mastering knife skills takes time, effort, patience, dexterity and maturity. You will need to allow your troopers plenty of time and opportunity to practise, practise, practise. Taking on simple projects is a great way to practise and hone skills.

 WARNING

Be sure to check the law regarding knives in your country before using a knife in public. The UK law is given at the back of this book on pages 204–205.

Knife and Tool Use Safety Brief:

Whenever you engage in a knife or tool skills activity with your troopers, use this simple safety brief:

1 Get a well-stocked first-aid kit.

- Include a designated, clearly labelled "cut box" that contains various size plasters
- Make sure troopers always know where the first-aid kit is.

2 Establish a "carving circle" or a safety zone around each trooper

- This is the diameter of their outstretched arms

- Make sure troopers know where the carving circles are
- When sitting, no other carver should be within another's circle

3 Troopers should always cut down and away from the body and gripping hand.

4 Troopers should never move from their carving spot with an unsheathed knife or tool. This saying may help your troopers to remember: *Sheath On Before You Move On.*

5 If troopers cut themselves, they must stop and let someone know straightaway, no matter how small the cut.

6 Troopers must take responsibility for their knife or tool. No one else.

7 Troopers must always take their time when using their knife and stay focused.

8 Carving can be tiring for novice hands. Make sure troopers know that if they get tired, they must take a rest.

9 When not in use, your knife must be sheathed. It must never be left on the floor, or stuck into a log or the ground.

10 Create a designated secure tool area. When tools and knives are finished with, they must be returned to this area.

The parts of your knife:

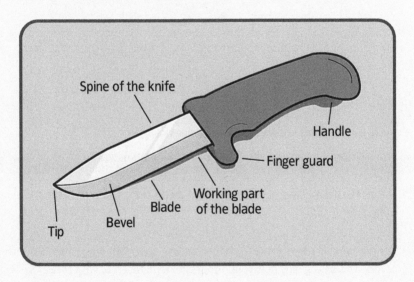

Safe ways to grip your knife for carving:

- **The Fist Grip.** This is a very secure grip and a great way to hold a knife. It will give users confidence when cutting or carving.

- **The Push Cut.** This is used for small cuts and gives a great deal of control over the knife.

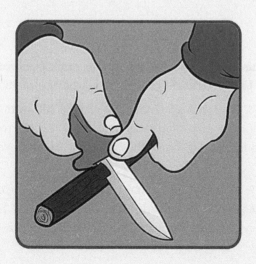

- **The Knee Brace.** This is a very safe and controlled way to use a knife. However, it does take practice to get used to the cut.

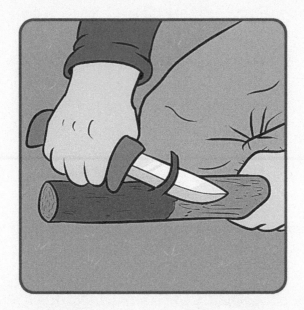

- **Splitting Cuts.** Used when splitting a stick, for example, to allow an arrow head to be placed in it or for cooking. There are two possible methods:

  - Method 1. Start with a Fist Grip, but grip the stick with your thumb and forefinger, and then apply downward pressure while rocking your knife back and forth. Using this method will only take the knife as deep as the blade

  - Method 2. Place the blade onto the top center of the stick, then baton the knife down using a thicker stick. Go to a depth of about 15 cm (6 in.), then remove and resheath your knife. Use your hands to complete the splitting of the stick.

MISSION ACCOMPLISHED

I verify that on this date .... I responsibly learned knife safety and skills with my Commando Dad.

Signed:

KEEPING YOUR KNIFE SHARP

Mission brief

- **Ground**: woods or forest
- **Situation**: you need to use a knife—but blunt knives can be dangerous
- **Mission**: to get a sharp edge on your knife
- **Skills**: dexterity, patience, hand–eye coordination

MISSION KEY

$ $ $ $ $ AGES 8+

this is intended for troopers to do themselves, under close supervision from Commando Dad

KIT LIST:

- A knife with a sheath
- Sharpening stone. Diamond stones are best for this job but search online for alternatives
- Flat surface (table or chopping board)
- An old leather belt
- Piece of paper—to test how sharp your blade is

WARNING

Be sure to check the law regarding knives in your country before using a knife in public. The UK law is given at the back of this book on pages 204–205.

INSTRUCTIONS:

1 For knife sharpening, we need to remove metal from both sides of the bevel to form a fine edge. This is known as our cutting edge.

2 **Set your stone up on a flat,** stable surface to start the sharpening process.

3 **Start with the knife placed on the end of the stone nearest to you,** with the cutting edge facing away from you and the finger guard part of the knife touching the edge of the stone. Tilt the knife until you achieve the correct bevel angle. You're now ready to start sharpening your knife.

4 **Move the knife away from you** up the stone, applying gentle pressure to the back of the blade with your fingers, and maintaining the angle as you progress towards the other end of the stone. As the blade moves up the stone, smoothly move the finger guard away from the side of the stone, so the whole blade and tip come into contact with the stone.

5 **Repeat this movement** from the bottom to the top of the stone for eight strokes.

6 **Turn the blade over and repeat** the movement for eight strokes, but this time, start from the far end of the stone and gently and carefully pull the blade towards the near end, again maintaining the correct bevel angle and moving the finger guard smoothly away from the stone.

7 **Alternate the push and pull strokes** across the stone for another eight strokes—four pushing away and four pulling towards. This allows you to keep the edge true to the center of the blade and maintain the balance of the knife.

8 **Focus your attention on the working part of the blade next,** because this is the area of the knife we use most for carving. Use the same eight strokes up and down the stone, but this time, the finger guard stays in contact with the stone throughout the movement.

9 **Repeat the eight alternate strokes.** These alternating sharpening strokes have created a very thin foil of metal where the bevels meet, and this is referred to as the burr. Visually check the burr by turning the bevel towards the light and angling the knife, checking for reflections from flat spots that indicate blunt areas. A sharp edge will reflect very little light.

10 The final process to create the perfect razor-sharp edge is to **strop your knife using a leather belt.** Feed the belt through the buckle around a tree branch, then hold the trailing end of the belt in your hand. Alternate brushing the knife backwards and forwards along the belt to remove any burr that may remain on the cutting edge. Fifty strokes should get your blade razor-sharp.

11 **Test the sharpness of your knife using your piece of paper.** If it's razor sharp, it should easily take the edge off the paper. Get into the good habit of keeping your knife sharp. There is a saying that you're only as sharp as your knife—so make sure you are a Sharp Commando Dad!

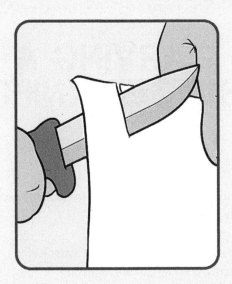

MISSION ACCOMPLISHED

I verify that on this date .... I carefully sharpened a knife with my Commando Dad.

Signed:

CARVING A BUTTER KNIFE

Mission brief

- **Ground**: enough space for each carver to have their own carving circle (see activity 2.13)
- **Situation**: calm, dry weather
- **Mission:** to use carving skills to create a butter knife
- **Skills**: dexterity, confidence, concentration

MISSION KEY

$ $ $ $ $ AGES 7+

KIT LIST:

- A knife with a sheath
- A piece of green hazel or sycamore, thumb-width and as long as your wrist to the top of your middle finger
- Comfortable seat in the trooper's carving circle (a log for example)
- A piece of sandpaper, to finish off the butter knife

INSTRUCTIONS:

1 **Using a fist grip, carefully start carving your stick,** taking off just small slithers of wood from one side. For larger pieces that need a bit more work, you can use the knee brace cut.

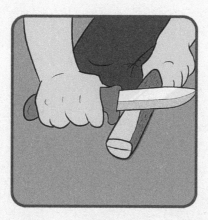

2 **Turn your stick over and carve the other side**. Again, take off small slithers and be careful not to cut too close to the center of the stick (known as the pith). Always cut away from your gripping hand.

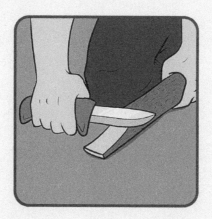

3 **Carve a rounded curved end** using the push cut at the tip of the butter knife.

4 **Turn the butter knife around and carve the handle**, rounding the ends with a push cut.

5 It's best to leave the wooden blade of your butter knife to dry for a week in a place that's cool and dry

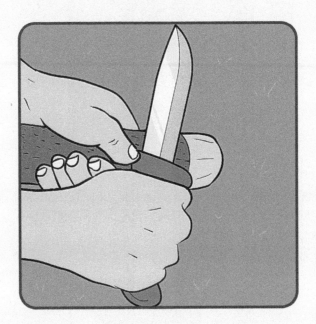

6 **Finish off** with a gentle sand down.

MISSION ACCOMPLISHED

I verify that on this date .... I carved a butter knife with my Commando Dad.

Signed:

FORAGING

Mission brief

- **Ground**: quiet areas of the wood
- **Situation**: autumn is best but free food is available all year around
- **Mission**: to find delicious fresh food
- **Skills**: identification, listening, comprehension

MISSION KEY

$ $ $ $ $ AGES 4+

KIT LIST:

- Non-slip shoes
- Long sleeves
- A bag to collect your foraged food—and one for each of your troopers
- Gloves

- Guide book to identify species (or your phone if your guide is online). Your troopers might appreciate one suitable for their age too

You'll be surprised at the abundance of edible food in nature—not just the obvious berries (which are hedgerow fruits) but also herbs, flowers, leaves and seeds.

GOLDEN RULES

1. Get a guide to edible foraging food so that you can identify what you can eat. Don't chance it—some species are poisonous. If in doubt, leave well alone. It is not possible to show you all the different species in this book but there are plenty of great resources available online—the UK's Woodland Trust provides guides by month and even recipes, for example.

2. Make sure your troops know that they never—ever—put anything in their mouth without checking with you first.

3. Only collect food where it is growing in abundance (which is why the quieter areas are good places to look).

4. Rare species must be left where they are—but do take a photo to share your treasure with others later!

5. Take only what you will eat—wildlife depends on wild food for survival. Don't just grab lots of everything and worry what to do with it later.

6. Know the law—you're only allowed to pick fruit for your own personal use (not to sell) if it is growing wild (not a commercial crop) and it's not on private land.

7. Pick carefully and do not damage plants. This includes not standing on plants to reach fruit or pulling on them (as this may uproot them).

8. If the area is popular with dog walkers, avoid plants at "dog pee" height.

INSTRUCTIONS:

1 **Plan your expedition**—what are you looking for? Where are you most likely to find it? It may be best to start with something you know will be growing in

abundance—weeds! There are plenty of recipes for dandelions and nettles for example (wear gloves for the latter as you need to grasp a nettle firmly to avoid being stung, but it's likely the troopers will be hesitant and you'll be on the hunt for dock leaves before you know it).

2 **Encourage the troopers to use all of their senses** and make it fun (who can find the first dandelion? Who can smell the wild garlic? What does that berry feel like?).

3 Depending on the age of your troopers, you might want to tell them about the flower fairies that live in the treetops and on the forest floor. You can find out all about them here: https://flowerfairies.com/meet-the-fairies/

4 **Be patient**—you may not find all (or any) of the plants you're looking for, but you will still have a great time outdoors in the fresh air with your troopers.

5 If you did find food, when you get home, gently wash it and lay it flat to dry, or if following a recipe, prepare as directed. Your troopers will love to help you prepare the food, so look for ways to get them involved while exercising all the necessary caution appropriate to their age.

6 I guarantee you that if your trooper has helped find, harvest, carry and cook foraged food, they will try it!

MISSION ACCOMPLISHED

I verify that on this date .... I foraged with my Commando Dad.

Signed:

SECTION 3:

MAKE

This section contains activities that will let your trooper's creative side run free.

The outdoors not only stimulates mental engagement and creativity but provides opportunities to incorporate the natural world into art projects. There are activities for troopers of all ages and opportunities for conservation crafts, such as making a bug hotel.

NATURE CROWN

Mission brief

- **Ground**: woods
- **Situation**: any time of year, but needs to be a dry day
- **Mission**: to create a crown fit for a king or queen of the woods
- **Skills**: imagination, dexterity, fine motor skills

MISSION KEY

$ $ $ $ $ AGES 3+

KIT LIST:

- Strip of firm card for each trooper—it can be as wide as you like. If your troopers are older, they may want to cut it into an interesting shape
- Scissors
- Sticky tape
- Glue

INSTRUCTIONS:

1. **Create the headband** for the crown using the card and secure the end using sticky tape. Test it on the head before decorating!

2. **Look for "treasure" to decorate the crown**—grass, twigs, flowers, leaves.

3. **Attach the treasure** to the crown using glue or sticky tape—depending on their age, your trooper can do this.

4. **Act regal.**

MISSION ACCOMPLISHED

I verify that on this date .... I made a nature crown with my Commando Dad.

Signed:

NATURE FRAME

Mission brief

- **Ground**: woods—all year round
- **Situation**: appreciating the beauty of the natural world
- **Mission**: to frame a work of natural art
- **Skills**: concentration, observation, communication

MISSION KEY

$ $ $ $ AGES 4+

KIT LIST:

- A frame. You can pick one up from a second-hand shop, or make your own using sticks from the forest floor and string or cord tied with overhand knots in each corner. See activity 2.3 for how to tie an overhand knot

- Camera or smartphone to record your trooper's works of art

The beauty of this activity is that no two pictures will ever be the same and it is an all-year-round activity. The frames will really help focus your trooper's attention and encourage close inspection. It's really important to get your troopers to explain their pictures to you—and for you to listen avidly.

INSTRUCTIONS:

There are two ways that you can use nature frames with your troopers:

1 Give your trooper a frame and ask them to "frame" something interesting. They can put it on the floor, hold it up to the sky, or against trees, etc. Get them to describe their work of art to you.

2 Troopers can also create nature pictures:
- Lay the frame on floor.
- Using natural materials on the woodland floor, create pictures.
- Get them to describe their works of art to you.

Take pictures of their artwork if you want a keepsake for later.

MISSION ACCOMPLISHED

I verify that on this date .... I made a nature frame with my Commando Dad.

Signed:

WILDERNESS BRACELETS

Mission brief

- **Ground**: dry woods with plenty to find on the forest floor
- **Situation**: walking through the woods
- **Mission**: to create a record of the day's adventures
- **Skills**: creativity, fine motor skills, communication

MISSION KEY

$ $ $ $ $ AGES 3+

KIT LIST:

- Sticky tape—the wider the better

INSTRUCTIONS:

1 **Make your troops a "bracelet"** with the tape—sticky side outwards.

2 Ask them to **find little items that will stick to it.** The rules are:

- It has to be found on the forest floor—no picking from trees or plants allowed.
- It has to be light.
- Absolutely no wildlife allowed!

3 **Snip off** the wristband for safe keeping.

4 When back at base camp use it to **recount the day's activities.**

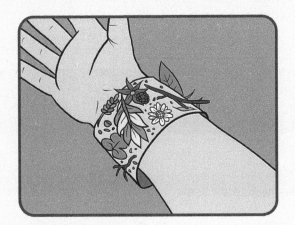

MISSION ACCOMPLISHED

I verify that on this date .... I made wilderness bracelets with my Commando Dad.

Signed:

LEAF PRINTING (TWO WAYS)

Mission brief

- **Ground**: forest, local park or garden
- **Situation**: spring and summer when the leaves are full of moisture are best for way 1, autumn is best for way 2
- **Mission**: to make a beautiful leaf print from your favorite leaves
- **Skills**: creativity, tool use, connecting with nature

MISSION KEY

$ $ $ $ $ AGES 4+

the first way involves tools, but the second way is suitable for troopers of any age

Way 1:
KIT LIST:

- Chopping board, or any hard surface to lean on
- Scissors
- Hammer, mallet or rounded stone you can pound with
- White cotton sheet
- Leaves

INSTRUCTIONS:

1 Using your scissors, **cut the sheet into squares**. The size of the squares is up to you, but 50 cm x 50 cm (20 in. x 20 in.) is a good size to go for.

2 Have the troopers collect leaves:

- Only take leaves from areas where there are lots of them.
- Avoid stinging or poisonous leaves—recce what you might find in the area you're planning to visit. "If in doubt, leave out!"
- Broad leaves are best, so tree leaves and dock leaves are good choices.
- You can also mix things up with buttercups and bracken.

3 Using your chopping board or other flat surface, **arrange your leaves** in whatever pattern you like—you can do it one at a time if you wish.

4 **Place your square of cotton over your leaves** and, using your mallet or hammer, repeatedly hit the leaf through the cotton.

5 Enjoy watching your print come to life.

Way 2:
KIT LIST:

- Chopping board, or any hard surface to lean on
- Scissors
- Paper
- Leaves
- Acrylic paints
- A rolling pin
- Paint brushes for each color paint you're using
- Palette or something you can mix paints on
- A plastic bag to bring used brushes home in

INSTRUCTIONS:

1 Have the troopers go and **collect leaves** that have fallen to the forest floor.

2 **Prepare your paint**—it should be the consistency of ketchup.

3 **Decide if you want the troopers to use one color** or if they can paint leaves in multiple colors.

4 **Give each trooper a piece of paper** (on a flat surface) and ask them to arrange their leaves onto it.

5 **Paint one leaf at a time.** The back side of the leaf is where you'll find the most interesting veins.

6 **Take the leaf and carefully place it on the piece of paper**—painted side down. Gently place another piece of paper on top.

7 Using the rolling pin, **firmly roll the leaf onto the paper**. The pressure will keep the leaf still and get a good, even image.

8 **Now paint another leaf** and so on, until the picture is finished.

9 **Have your troopers help you tidy up**—no painted leaves or brushes should be left in the great outdoors.

10 Make sure that you **properly wash your brushes** when you get back to base camp, before the paint dries. Wash them in warm soapy water, rubbing the brush in circles on the palm of your hand to really get the paint out. When the paint is gone, rinse well, squeeze dry, reshape the brush and leave to dry. Troopers may like to help with this activity. If that's the case, it may be a good idea to put the warm soapy water in buckets and wash the brushes outside.

MISSION ACCOMPLISHED

I verify that on this date .... I did leaf printing with my Commando Dad.

Signed:

TREE RUBBING

Mission brief

- **Ground**: anywhere with trees, including your garden
- **Situation**: any time of year
- **Mission**: to explore, and appreciate, the patterns and textures of bark
- **Skills**: literacy, dexterity, creativity

MISSION KEY

$ $ $ $ $ AGES 2+

KIT LIST:

- Trees
- Paper—thinner paper will show the pattern better
- Different colored wax crayons

Tree rubbing is a simple and creative way to help children learn about patterns and textures, as well as getting them to notice how bark differs among different species of trees. It can also help children learn about the different parts and characteristics of trees.

INSTRUCTIONS:

1 **Explain the task,** telling the troopers that the trees that make the best patterns are gnarly, bumpy and rugged (this is a good opportunity to introduce them to words they may not have heard before).

2 **Ask your troopers to choose a tree** and explore the bark with their hands. Ask them how it feels. If there's more than one tree, they can explore a few and pick a favorite.

3 **Give them a piece of paper** and tell them to hold it against the bark with one hand while rubbing the crayon over the paper with the other. Troopers can decide if they want to do one tree per piece of paper or to make a collage of different trees.

Your troopers may be interested to know that a tree's bark is very similar to our own skin. One of its key jobs is to protect the tree from hot sun, drying winds, infection, insects, hungry birds and even animals. But some determined animals manage to get to the bark, or the wood beneath. Mammals like to eat bark, so if you or your trooper see bite marks, you might be able to work out what animals have been in the area.

MISSION ACCOMPLISHED

I verify that on this date .... I took some tree rubbings with my Commando Dad.

Signed:

BUG HOTEL

Mission brief

- **Ground**: the woods in autumn are particularly good for materials such as dry grass and hollow plant stems
- **Situation**: all year round, but in autumn, when mini-beasts are looking for a place to hibernate, is particularly good
- **Mission**: to create a bug hotel to help the wildlife on your doorstep
- **Skills**: using a range of materials for construction, conservation, dexterity

MISSION KEY

$ $ $ $ $ AGES 4+

KIT LIST:

- Your bug hotel will need a sturdy frame separated into compartments and a roof to keep the contents dry. For the frame, used wooden pallets are perfect—try asking at industrial areas, supermarkets or small businesses for these.

- You will need to create smaller compartments in your frame by recycling old materials you already have. For example:
  - Old housebricks with holes
  - Old roofing tiles
  - Stones
  - Broken plant pots

- Sections of drainpipe
- Canes
- Corrugated cardboard
- To fill the smaller compartments you've created, you will need to use natural materials you can find on the woodland floor to create warm, dry, safe places for creepy crawlies to hide. Good materials include:
  - Twigs

- Dead wood
- Dry grass
- Moss
- Dry leaves
- Bark
- Pine cones
- Acorn cups
- Hollow stems

This activity takes place at base camp but you will need a sortie into the woods for the natural materials to furnish your bug hotel before it opens for business.

INSTRUCTIONS:

1 Work out with your troopers where in your garden or yard your bug hotel will be built. As a rule of thumb, bugs like cooler, moist places to shelter but if you want to attract solitary bees, look for a sunnier spot.

2 **Build your frame** and create layers using your recycled materials.

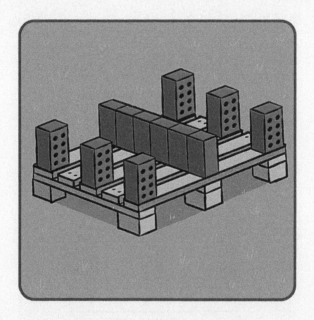

3 **Use the natural materials from the forest floor to fill the compartments you've created.** There are no hard and fast rules, but everything does need to be packed in tightly but not squashed. The idea is to create tiny nooks and crannies.

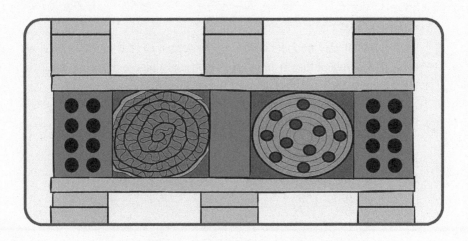

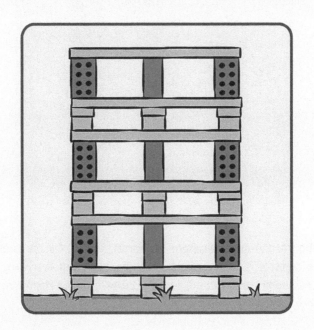

4 **Create a roof for your hotel** using old tiles or wood.

Why build a bug hotel?

Building a bug hotel will continue to help your troopers engage with nature and the environment, and for older troopers you can talk about sustainability and conservation. Your troopers will be helping to provide mini-beasts with a safe place to shelter, lay their eggs, raise their young, and hide from predators. In turn they will pollinate flowers and help to keep your gardens free from pests.

What guests can you expect?

The type of guests that visit your hotel will depend on the materials you use:

- Dead wood and bark will attract beetles, centipedes, woodlice and spiders
- Hollow stems are good for solitary bees to lay their eggs in
- Straw and dry grass attract a wide variety of insects that will burrow and hibernate
- Dry leaves will attract Ladybugs looking to hibernate over the winter
- Corrugated cardboard is great for lacewings

MISSION ACCOMPLISHED

I verify that on this date .... I built a bug hotel with my Commando Dad.

Signed:

CHRISTMAS TREE DECORATION

Mission brief

- **Ground**: woodland floor in autumn
- **Situation**: a bare Christmas tree
- **Mission**: to make Christmas tree decorations for base camp, or as gifts for loved ones
- **Skills**: dexterity; imagination; creativity

MISSION KEY

$ $ $ $ $ AGES 3+

KIT LIST:

- Pine cones
- Old toothbrush (for cleaning)
- Newspaper or an old sheet
- Glue

- Craft paint
- Paint brushes
- String or ribbon

INSTRUCTIONS:

1 **Collect your pine cones** from the woodland floor but only as many as you intend to use as mini-beasts make their homes in them.

2 When back at base camp **clean the pinecones thoroughly** with an old toothbrush. Best to do this outside in case any bugs slipped under the radar.

3 Cover your table with old newspaper and **paint the pinecones**.

4 **Leave them to dry.**

5 **Attach a string or ribbon** to the top of the cone with glue so that they can be hung from the tree. If using a ribbon, write the year inside so that you (or the recipient if giving them as a gift) will always be able to remember when it was made.

Ideas for decorating:

- Paint the whole pine cone in one color (more than that and it can get messy)
- Add glue to the tips and add glitter or mini pom-poms
- Just paint the edges of the pine cone—white can be effective as it looks like snow
- Make characters and creatures using other things found on the forest floor

MISSION ACCOMPLISHED

I verify that on this date .... I made Christmas tree decorations with my Commando Dad.

Signed:

3D MAP MAKING

Mission brief

- **Ground**: any natural space with lots of features for your 3D map (see sticky note below)
- **Situation**: an important object has gone missing—and needs to be found
- **Mission**: to guide troopers to a specific location using your 3D map
- **Skills**: map building, resource collection, observation

MISSION KEY

$ $ $ $ $ AGES 5+

KIT LIST:

- Whatever resources you can find on the ground
- 4 x straight wooden logs to mark out your map area about 1 m (3 ft) in length
- 1 x small bunch of keys
- 1 x single key

WARNING:

Never, ever, use keys that you actually need for this activity. This is for all those spare keys that are lurking in kitchen drawers and on keyrings.

A 3D map is a dynamic, tactile representation of an area. For example, if you are putting a tree on your 3D map, it needs to stand up like a tree. For a hole, you dig a hole. You can use stones to show certain features like the line of a path.

INSTRUCTIONS:

This activity can be done either individually, or as pairs if you want to introduce teamwork. Ideally, you need to produce two maps so that troopers have the opportunity to both hide and seek the keys.

1 **Instruct each trooper, or pair, to explore** and carefully observe a particular part of the woods, taking in as much information as they possibly can. They need to pay particular attention to features that stick out to them. For example, are there particular trees that are big or a funny shape? Are there any paths, streams or hedge lines? Are there any features like fire pits, shelters or seating areas?

2 When the troopers are confident they could capture the main features of the area in a map, have them **gather as many resources as they need** from the forest floor to create it.

3 **Help them to mark out** their 1 m x 1 m (3 ft x 3 ft) area with the logs. This is the boundary of their 3D map.

4 **Troopers create a 3D map of their surroundings.** They could even come up with interesting names for features on their map, such as "wiggly path," "nobbly bobbly tree," etc.

5 Once all maps are complete, **it's time to play hide and seek**.

6 Each trooper, or pair, now needs to go and **hide the small bunch of keys** in their surroundings.

7 They then **mark the location of the hidden keys on their 3D map** using the single key.

8 When Commando Dad says "Go!" the other team needs to see if they can **find the missing keys using the 3D map**.

9 Once the keys have been located, the teams can **swap roles**.

MISSION ACCOMPLISHED

I verify that on this date .... I found my way with a 3D map with my Commando Dad.

Signed:

BOW AND ARROWS

Mission brief

- **Ground:** woodland is always best, but any outdoor space, such as a park or garden
- **Situation:** the group is hungry for food and needs protection
- **Mission:** make a bow and arrow to protect and feed everyone
- **Skills:** tree/wood identification, safe tool use, hand–eye coordination

MISSION KEY

$ $ $ $ $ AGES 5+

KIT LIST:

- Sheath knife or penknife
- Gardening glove, for hand protection
- Sticks suitable for a bow and some arrows (see instructions)
- Elastic (best if you plan to use arrows) or string
- Tin cans for target practice
- Secateurs (optional)
- Potato peeler for bark stripping (optional)

INFO

Safety is always paramount. You know your troopers best, and you must be satisfied that they are capable of handling tools. You must always keep them under close supervision. For younger troopers, you can handle the tools, but always explain to them what you're doing and how you are making sure you are being safe.

INSTRUCTIONS:

Whenever using either knives or tools, be sure to **give your troopers a safety brief** (see activity 2.10) and an explanation about each of the pieces of equipment they will be using. Show them the cutting edge, **demonstrate safe use**, how to safely carry and how to safely hand over each tool to another trooper.

Your location needs to have:

- Plenty of fallen sticks on the ground.
- Plenty of space for your potential hunters to run around.

Once fully briefed, have your troopers **find suitable sticks** for bows and arrows on the woodland floor. Absolutely no cutting from trees is allowed.

- **Bow:** troopers need to find a stick that is comfortable to handle, bendy and has a natural crescent-shape to it. Ideal types of wood are hazel or young ash.
- **Arrows:** troopers must find shorter straight sticks.

Making bows:

- Sit troopers in their carving circles.
- **Stripping your bow:** If the troopers want to strip the outer rough bark away to make their bow white and smooth, they can do this with a potato peeler. For younger troopers, you will need to do this for them.
- **Stringing your bow:** Using either a sheath knife or a penknife, cut a notch on either end of your bow. The cut will need to be on the outer side—opposite to where the elastic or string will go.

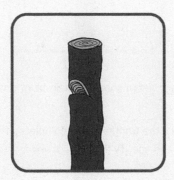

- In the notches, tightly tie on your length of string or elastic—this connects the two ends of your bow together. A simple double overhand knot will be perfect for attaching the string to the notch. See activity 2.3 for information on how to tie an overhand knot.
  - Supervise older troopers if you are confident they can handle a penknife or sheath knife safely.
  - You must perform this part of the bow-making process for younger troopers.
  - Whoever is cutting—they must always work away from their body.
- **Making the arrows:** If you want to strip the outer bark from the arrow sticks so that they're nice and smooth, use the potato peeler as before.

- A notch needs to be cut across the end of each arrow, using the sheath or pen knife. This will hold the elastic or string in place when the arrow is pulled back for launching.

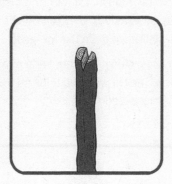

- The front end of each arrow should remain blunt and not ever be sharpened into a point.

- **Target practice:** Once the troopers have completed their bow and arrows, give them a safety brief and specify the rules of engagement for playing with bows and arrows:

  ○ Troopers must never, ever, aim an arrow at another trooper.

  ○ Arrows must only ever be aimed at the targets that have been set up around the woods.

- Have the troopers help you to set up two or three mini-ranges around the woods using tin cans. For example, line tin cans up along a log, place them in tree branches, on top of rocks, etc.

- Make sure the troopers know that if they successfully hit a target, they must return it to its starting point before moving onto the next range.

- Always collect up all tin cans at the end of the game and take them home to base camp.

Tip: Using clean tin cans for target practice is a great idea, as they're a good size and weight, and make a gratifying sound when you hit them.

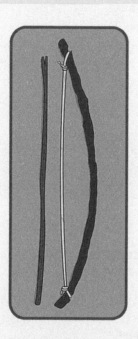

MISSION ACCOMPLISHED

I verify that on this date .... I made a bow and arrow with my Commando Dad.

Signed:

MAKE A CATAPULT

Mission brief

- **Ground:** the great outdoors, but if the wood is fresh, it will need to be dried out at base camp
- **Situation:** a controlled environment on a day with clear visibility
- **Mission:** to create a catapult and practise shooting accuracy
- **Skills:** communication, dexterity, hand–eye coordination

MISSION KEY

$ $ $ $ $ AGES 5+

KIT LIST:

- Catapult frame, usually a small tree branch with a V-shaped fork that can fit in the hand comfortably. The "V" shape must be wide enough to have ammo pass through—at least 30 degrees

- Elastic bands. Latex rubber surgical tubing is best, as it is readily available online and it won't snap. You can buy these complete with pouches online too. Look for "latex catapult rubber band"

- If drying the wood:
  - Microwave
  - Paper towel roll
  - Plastic bag
- Dental floss
- Saw for cutting small branches
- Knife for making notches and cutting narrow latex tubing
- Empty tin cans (for target practice in the great outdoors)

WARNING

If you want to use your catapult for target practice, then you might choose to use stones as ammo. In this instance, close supervision by you is essential. Never let your trooper fire at another trooper or you—but this is especially true when using stones. Remember the story of David and Goliath? The catapult was even recognized as a deadly weapon in the ancient world—Romans had special pinchers that could remove an embedded stone fired from a catapult from the bodies of soldiers. Even if you have a pair of these to hand, exercise extreme caution.

INSTRUCTIONS:
Build your catapult:

1. **Find your catapult frame.** I advocate finding one on the ground rather than cutting it off a tree. It can be hard to know if it's the right shape for you without holding it in your hand, making foraging the best option. However, if you need to cut one from a tree, look for low-hanging branches and use a suitable saw to cut it safely from the tree.

2. **Ensure your catapult frame is dry.** Wood needs to be dry and rigid for an effective catapult. If your wood has been cut directly from the tree, or not been on the ground long, it will still have sap in it. You can either take the wood back to base camp and store it for later, or dry it yourself. The quickest method is to use a microwave:

- **Wipe the frame** with a dry cloth or paper towel roll (do not use anything wet as this will defeat the purpose).

- **Wrap it in clean paper towel roll and place in a plastic bag** but do not seal it completely. The bag will not only help you gauge when the moisture has disappeared but also protect your microwave—and future meals—from odd tastes and smells.

- On high, **microwave your frame for 30 seconds** and take it out and unwrap it. Let it cool for 10 minutes, then rewrap and repeat. Replace the paper towel roll when it gets too damp and wipe out any moisture from the inside of the plastic bag.

- **Repeat until there is no moisture.** You will be able to tell this in two ways: no hissing and no new moisture on the paper towel.

3 **Carve notches.** You need to carve a notch around the top of each branch of your V to ensure your elastic fits snugly.

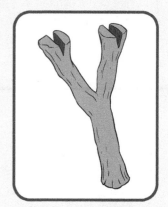

4 **Cut the elastic.** There is an art to this. The elastic needs to be long enough to draw back but not so long that it loses power. Cut elastic with a knife.

5 **Attach the elastic** by sliding the ends through the notches in the top of each branch of your V, then a little way down the front side of the catapult. Secure with dental floss, which has very strong properties. Tie it as tight as you can and cut the loose ends.

Target practice:

Use clean tin cans for target practice as they're a good size and weight, and make a gratifying sound when you hit them. Make sure you don't place tin cans in front of anything breakable as the ammo can easily ricochet.

Suitable ammo:

In and around base camp:

- Marshmallows.
- Ping pong balls.
- Dry sponge.
- Soft balls.

Great outdoors:

- Acorns.
- Horse chestnuts.
- Pebbles and stones (but only under close supervision from Commando Dad).

Ammo in base camp needs to be soft and light. My daughter is still a crack shot with small cuddly toys. When using heavier ammo in the great outdoors, make sure your trooper understands that they are in charge of their catapult at all times and be sure to give a trooper boundary brief. Make it clear that absolutely NO negligent discharge will be tolerated.

MISSION ACCOMPLISHED

I verify that on this date .... I started a journey to becoming a crack shot with my Commando Dad.

Signed:

MAKE A ROPE SWING

Mission brief

- **Ground:** woods, or garden if you have a suitable tree
- **Situation:** a large, strong tree with a clear area at its base (so those on the rope can swing without coming into contact with anything) and a branch at least 16 cm (6 in.) thick
- **Mission:** to make—and use—a rope swing. If you are on private land, seek permission
- **Skills:** construction, self-confidence, self-esteem

MISSION KEY

Construction:

Swinging:

$ $ $ $ $ AGES 6+

KIT LIST:

- Laid rope, at least 2.5 cm (1 in.) thick

- String or cord to help get the rope over the branch

- A counterweight to help get the string or cord over the branch. A padlock is ideal

- Gaffer or electrical tape to cap the cut end of the rope

- A log or small branch if you'd like to incorporate a seat. This must be small enough to sit on comfortably, while being thick enough to support the heaviest person's weight

WARNING

It is vital that you carry out your trooper boundary brief for this mission. Please exercise caution, common sense and close supervision to ensure troopers are a safe distance away from you when you throw the counterweight into the tree, and are subsequently able to enjoy their rope swing without hurting themselves unnecessarily. Bumps, scrapes and bruises are par for the course, but bad sprains and breaks must be avoided.

INSTRUCTIONS:

For instructions on how to tie these knots—with the exception of the double constrictor knot—see activity 2.3.

1. **Reconnaissance (recce)**. If possible, find the best tree before you set out on the mission. This will enable you to get directly to the task in hand when your troopers are there, and gauge the length of the rope you'll need so you can cut it back at base camp.

2. **Tie a bowline knot towards the end of your rope**. It is a sturdy and reliable knot that will secure the rope swing to the branch. **NB**—If you want to strip out your swing later on, make sure to attach a double length of string through your bowline loop while it is at ground level. By pulling on these strings, you will be able to loosen off the loop when it is at the top and draw the rope down again to take it off the branch.

3. **Put a figure-of-eight stopper knot underneath** the bowline to ensure it doesn't come undone.

4. **Wrap gaffer tape around the end of the rope to prevent fraying.**

⑤ Get your rope swing over the chosen branch: at the other end of the rope (the one without knots), attach the string or cord to the counterweight and with a simple overhand knot (see diagram below). You can secure the knot further with more gaffer tape. Throw your counterweight over the branch so that it takes the rope around the branch and down to you. You can now remove the counterweight.

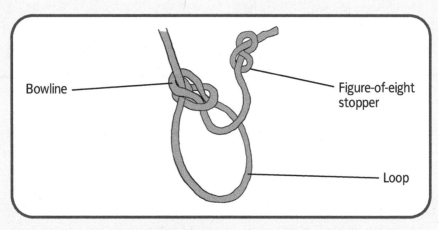

Bowline — Figure-of-eight stopper

Loop

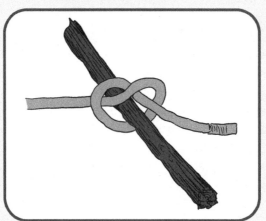

6 **Thread the end of the rope without knots through the bowline.** This will form a loop. Then pull, and keep pulling until the loop is tight around the branch above.

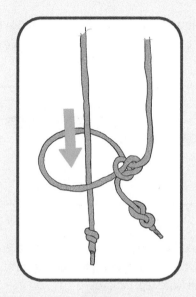

7 You now have a basic swing. **Make two big overhand knots** in the bottom of the rope to create "riding turns" which you can stand or sit on, and **wrap gaffer tape around the end of the rope to prevent fraying.**

8 **Construct a seat.** If you'd like a seat, fasten a suitable piece of wood to the rope with a double constrictor knot, a simple and secure binding knot.

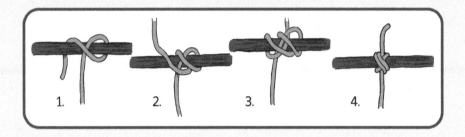

1.   2.   3.   4.

- Wrap the rope around your piece of wood with an overhand action, bringing the working part of the rope left over the standing part, and halfway over the piece of wood again (see step 1 above).

- Bring the working end the rest of the way around the piece of wood (see step 2), and wrap it over and under again, to make an "X" shape with a double line on one side. Then thread the working end under the two loops and up through the top part of the "X" shape (see step 3). Pull the working end and standing part to tighten and you have your constrictor knot (step 4).

- Use your gaffer or electrical tape to cap the end of your rope to finish it off, so it doesn't fray.

9 **Test your swing**—a task for Commando Dad—sit on the swing seat (without swinging at first) to ensure all knots are holding. Once you are satisfied that your swing is safe, just confirm that there are no previously unseen obstacles that could get in the way when you swing.

10 Swing!

MISSION ACCOMPLISHED

I verify that on this date .... I made a rope swing with my Commando Dad.

Signed:

MINI-RAFT RACE

Mission brief

- **Ground:** can be prepared at base camp
- **Situation:** sunny day at a shallow stream
- **Mission:** to create a mini-raft that floats on water
- **Skills:** construction, water safety, competition

MISSION KEY

$ $ $ $ $

AGES 5+
with your help

KIT LIST:

- Large, straight twigs (see instructions for details)
- String
- Knife or scissors
- Pencil
- PVA or wood glue

WARNING

Please always exercise great caution when near water with your troopers, especially if they are unable to swim. These instructions also include using a knife or scissors to cut string. Please exercise common sense and close supervision if you intend to let your troopers undertake this task.

INSTRUCTIONS:

1 **Gather straight twigs.** Bumps will give you a holey raft, so aim for the straightest ones you can find.

2 Snap them into roughly the same length—**about 20–30-cm (8–12-in.) lengths**.

3 **Put a stick horizontally in front of you and lay a twig on top of it at one end.**

4 Tie **an overhand knot** around the first twig (see activity 2.3) and then

continue to **loop** the string around each twig in a cross fashion (see diagram), **finishing off with another overhand knot.**

5 **Repeat** on the opposite edge.

6 **Secure the knots** by gluing a wooden stick over the top (both sides). Allow to dry.

7 Troopers write their names on the lolly sticks to identify which raft belong to whom.

8 **Race your rafts:**

- Find a suitable launch point in the stream: all troopers need to be able to walk easily through the stream.
- Place the rafts in the stream and let the current take them.
- Determine a point for the end of the race.
- The first raft to the end point wins.
- Any dispute over raft ownership can be resolved by reading the names on the lolly sticks.

MISSION ACCOMPLISHED

I verify that on this date .... I sailed a raft across the rapids with my Commando Dad.

Signed:

SECTION 4:

PLAY

This section contains games that are suitable for playing outdoors. All games work whether it is just you and your trooper, or larger groups.

Troopers have a biological drive to play—it is how they explore their environment, and it aids their mental, physical, emotional and social development. If you join in, you will make play even better for your troopers. However, this doesn't mean taking part half-heartedly or awkwardly; throw yourself in! You will be amazed how good it feels.

"ONE-TWO-THREE... WHERE ARE YOU?"

Mission brief

- **Ground**: woods, forest, local park
- **Situation**: the woods are an easy place to get lost, so we need to have a way of finding each other
- **Mission**: to find missing troopers using our voices and ears
- **Skills**: establishing boundaries, building trust, listening

MISSION KEY

$ $ $ $ $ AGES 3+

KIT LIST:

- Dark-colored clothes if you have them, to make finding each other more challenging—but anything dark will be fine

This is a great warm-up game for your troopers, getting them physically active and engaged with their environment. It also helps establish rules of how to avoid getting lost and how to find each other if your troopers become separated and cannot see each other. Troopers can do this activity individually, but it's a great team game.

INSTRUCTIONS:

1 **Divide your group into two teams**; if a team is made up of younger troopers it will need to have an adult supervisor.

2 **Team One goes off and hides** out of sight.

3 **Team Two seeks them** by shouting "One-Two-Three… Where Are You?" until they hear the reply "One-Two-Three… We're Over Here!"

4 Team Two needs to **move towards the area they hear the reply from,** repeating the call and using the answers to refine the search until they find the other team.

5 **Repeat this game,** while reinforcing the rules of keeping in contact with each other within a woodland setting.

MISSION ACCOMPLISHED

I verify that on this date .... I used the "One-Two-Three...
Where Are You?" method to find the hidden troopers with my Commando
Dad.

Signed:

ASSAULT COURSE

Mission brief

- **Ground:** park, large garden or any wide open space
- **Situation:** you need to get from A to B quickly—but there are many obstacles in your path
- **Mission:** to get round the assault course as fast as you can. For park-based assault courses, choose a day when the park is likely to be empty (cold or rainy days, for example) to stop innocent victims getting caught in the crossfire
- **Skills:** hand–eye coordination, physical activity, self-esteem

MISSION KEY

$ $ $ $ $ AGES 5+

KIT LIST:

- Trainers with a good grip
- Old, battle-hardened clothes that are OK to adventure in
- Waterproof notepad—you can pick these up from any camping shop
- Pencil
- Whistle

For an improvised assault course:

- Suitable equipment you could carry from base camp: hula hoops, skipping ropes, bats and balls, a scramble net or tarp and pegs, a bucket, etc.

- Suitable equipment you can find in the environment, such as benches, trees, bushes, etc.

INSTRUCTIONS:

1 **Check the course for potential hazards:** broken glass, items hidden in the grass, sharp edges, animal poo, etc.

2 **If using an improvised course, set up the course with your troops.** Obstacles will be dependent on the ability of your troopers and the space available. Here are some ideas to get you started:

- Hula hoop: troopers have to pick up the hula hoop, and do a couple of full spins.

- Skipping rope: troopers can either complete a prescribed set of skips, or it can be laid on the ground for a tightrope walk.

- Commando crawl: troopers have to crawl on their stomachs underneath a tarpaulin or scramble net that's been staked down on the grass.

- Ball skills: throw balls into a bucket (the balls can be different sizes and the bucket further away for different abilities).

- Physical Training (PT): use the space by having troopers run from A to B, or do cartwheels or forward rolls.

3 **Ensure you have a finish line** for everyone to aim for.

4 **When the course is set up, brief the troops.** Ideally, give them a demonstration yourself and ensure everyone is clear and understands what's expected.

5 Set the troops off one at a time, while you and the rest of the unit shout encouragement.

6 **Ask a trooper to time you** as you do the course.

7 **Record everyone's time in the notepad.** This gives everyone the opportunity to discover their personal best—and exceed it.

For a park assault course:
Find a park with suitable equipment: slides, monkey bars,
climbing frames and walls, firemen's poles, etc.

MISSION ACCOMPLISHED

I verify that on this date .... I set a PB (personal best) time on the assault course with my Commando Dad.

Commando Dad's PB time: .... My PB time: ....

Signed:

CAMO CHALLENGE

Mission brief

- **Ground**: woods or forest with plenty of ground cover
- **Situation:** a predator is approaching and you need to blend in with your surroundings
- **Mission:** you must disappear from sight
- **Skills**: camouflage, observation, stillness

MISSION KEY

$ $ $ $ $ AGES 5+

KIT LIST:

- Cam cream or face paint to disguise the face and hands. You can buy cam cream (which is a type of face paint) at camping or fishing shops, but face paints are just as effective

- Baby wipes for cleaning up after your mission is complete.

- Camera to capture how well the unit blended in.

- Dark boots or rubber boots (which can be edged with foliage).

- Old, battle-hardened clothes that are OK to adventure in

- A dark coat, with a hood if possible

- Large, thick elastic bands to attach foliage the body. Ensure they are not too tight as they will cause discomfort

- Brash: foliage from the forest floor—select carefully. Avoid spines and stingers

This is a good activity when entertaining troopers from other units.

> ⚠️ **WARNING**
>
> Don't <u>ever</u> use boot polish as cam cream. It is oil-based and will resist all but the most rigorous attempts to remove it.

INSTRUCTIONS:

Use a buddy system throughout the task as troopers will need to help each other to succeed.

1. **Make your way into the woods.** Encourage troopers to look around them and take note of the changes they see in the colors of the plants, trees, leaves and the ground.

2. **When it's time to begin, break out the cam cream or face paints.** Buddies put cam cream on each other's faces, ensuring a good covering especially on cheekbones, noses and foreheads. Finish with ears and neck.

NOT ENOUGH   JUST RIGHT   TOO MUCH

3 **Troopers put three or four elastic bands around their arms and legs and take it in turns to disguise each other.** This involves pushing brash under the bands, continuing to do so until the trooper looks like a bush. More elastic bands can be added. Make sure the bands aren't too tight around the arms and legs of your troopers.

4 Foliage should also be stuffed into boots. It's important that the trooper should still be able to move around—not least because their next task is to disguise their buddy.

5 **Time to test your camouflage.** The most effective way to test your camouflage is to put it into action, with a game such as Hide and Seek Commando Style (activity 4.6 below).

This is a great activity for encouraging teamwork. It also helps the whole unit to pay attention to the environment around them, and to improvise, adapt and overcome in order to find what they need to blend in.

MISSION ACCOMPLISHED

I verify that on this date .... I learned how to hide in plain sight with my Commando Dad.

Signed:

ROCK, PAPER, SCISSORS: COMMANDO STYLE

Mission brief

- **Ground**: woods or forest, but can be played in the park
- **Situation**: you're facing an enemy that wants to steal your troopers
- **Mission**: to defeat the other team with your object choices
- **Skills**: teamwork, communication, co-operation

MISSION KEY

$ $ $ $ AGES 3+

KIT LIST:

- No kit required for this game

For this game, we need a minimum of six players, plus two adults (one per team).

INSTRUCTIONS:

1 **Explain the basic rules** of rock, paper, scissors:

- Rock beats scissors by blunting them.
- Scissors beat paper by cutting it.
- Paper beats rock by wrapping around it.

2 **Show the group how to create each of the items** using their bodies:

- Rock is made by squatting on the ground and covering your head with your hands.
- Paper is made by your arms being stretched straight above your head.
- Scissors are made by stretching your arms out in front of you and clapping your hands together.

3 **Divide the group into two teams** with one adult per team.

4 Each team decides which of the three objects they are going to be.

5 The two teams face one another and on the count of three they each become their chosen object.

6 The winning team from that round gets to steal a member from the opposite team.

7 The team that ends up with all the players wins.

An alternative points system could be the winning team wins a point and the first team to reach five points wins.

MISSION ACCOMPLISHED

I verify that on this date .... I played a game of rock, paper, scissors—commando style—with my Commando Dad.

Signed:

TROOPER TAIL GRAB

This game requires a minimum of six players.

Mission brief:

- **Ground**: woods or forest, but any open space is fine
- **Situation:** you have a tail and you want to keep it away from predators
- **Mission:** to keep your own tail safe while grabbing the other tails
- **Skills**: dexterity, speed, stealth

MISSION KEY

$ $ $ $ $ AGES 4+

KIT LIST:

- Strips of fabric to make the tails

INSTRUCTIONS:

1. Each player takes a fabric tail that they tuck into the back of their pants.

2. Commando Dad tells all troopers how they will need to move when the game starts—for example, "Walk like you're on the moon," "Walk like an elephant" or "Walk like you're sneaking downstairs to see if Santa has been."

3. Commando Dad shouts "go" and troopers move as directed.

4. When Commando Dad shouts "tail grab!" each trooper has 10 seconds to grab a tail from another trooper while avoiding losing their own.

5 **If a trooper does lose their tail they are out of the game,** unless they can grab another tail before the 10 seconds is up.

6 **The winner is the trooper left with their own tail,** and with the greatest number of tails they've captured from others.

MISSION ACCOMPLISHED

I verify that on this date .... I played trooper tail grab with my Commando Dad.

Signed:

MISSION 4.6

HIDE AND SEEK: COMMANDO STYLE

Mission brief

- **Ground**: anywhere, but woods have excellent hiding places
- **Situation**: enemies are all around
- **Mission**: to get back to the base camp undetected
- **Skills**: camouflage, silent movement, observation

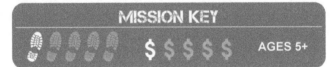

MISSION KEY

$ $ $ $ $ AGES 5+

KIT LIST:

- Can be played in any clothes, but if the players really want to improve their chances of not being detected, they can camouflage themselves— see activity 4.3 for guidance

INSTRUCTIONS:

1. **The rally point serves as base**—this helps reinforce where your troopers return to if you need them all back.

2. **Choose a seeker.**

3. **The seeker counts to 20 slowly** while the rest of the players hide. Twenty is a good number because players must remain within earshot for the game to be effective and the relatively short time encourages them to hide nearby.

4. **Once the seeker gets to 20, they must leave the base.** All hiders must stay still, exactly where they are.

5. **When the seeker finds his first hider, they shout "Twos Up!"** meaning there are now two seekers. The seekers can choose whether to stay close together or set off in different directions.

6. **This is the cue for all other hiders to get back to base camp** before being detected by an ever-growing number of seekers. The less risky strategy is get on the move and get back to base without being spotted.

7. **Every time a seeker finds another hider they must shout out the number** ("Threes Up!" "Fours Up!" and so on).

8. **If a hider breaks cover and runs for base, as long as they can get there without being touched by a seeker, they are safe.** They then must shout "One safe at base!" (and subsequently "Two safe at base!" etc.) so that everyone in the game can keep count of how many are safe, how many are seeking and how many are still hiding.

9 **The first one back at base is the ultimate winner**, and they can either choose to be the seeker in the next game or nominate another player.

MISSION ACCOMPLISHED

I verify that on this date .... I played hide and seek— commando style—with my Commando Dad.

Signed:

HORSE CHESTNUTS

Mission brief

- **Ground:** near a horse chestnut tree around mid to late September
- **Situation:** horse chestnuts are everywhere
- **Mission:** to take a humble horse chestnut and help it realize its potential for horse chestnut mastery
- **Skills:** identification, dexterity, patience

MISSION KEY

$ $ $ $ $ AGES 4+

KIT LIST:

- Horse chestnuts
- Plastic bag or tub (for collection)
- Washing-up bowl or bucket of water (for selection)
- Newspaper (for protection)
- A meat skewer or Phillips-head screwdriver
- 30 cm (12 in.) of string per horse chestnut
- Sticky tape
- 120 ml (4 fl. oz.) vinegar
- A jug

WARNING

These instructions include using a skewer or thin screwdriver for boring holes in horse chestnuts, and this activity should only be undertaken by Commando Dad.

Horse chestnuts get much harder with age so make sure troopers keep their champions for next season. A forward-thinking trooper can store some for the following year. Just make sure you bore a hole in them first—no need for vinegar. Ageing will do the work.

INSTRUCTIONS:

Hardening horse chestnuts is the stuff of folklore and you may have your own method of gaining a tactical advantage. Here's the one that worked for me as a trooper:

1 **Gather horse chestnuts** to take back to base camp.

2 **Break open the prickly green cases** and look for horse chestnuts that are:

- Uncracked
- Firm
- Symmetrical

3 Take your selected horse chestnuts and **drop them in the bowl or bucket of water**. If they float they have some damage inside and unfortunately do not have the potential to become champions. Discard.

4 Take your "sinkers" and put them through their paces:
- Pour the vinegar into a jug
- Drop your horse chestnuts in
- Leave to soak

5 Twenty-four hours later, **remove the horse chestnuts from the vinegar and leave them to dry** on a newspaper on the kitchen counter.

6 When dry, **bore a hole through each** using a meat skewer or a thin screwdriver. Take your string and wrap a piece of sticky tape around the end (like you see on a shoelace), as this will help with threading.

7 **Thread your piece of string through the horse chestnut and tie in a knot.**

THE RULES OF PLAYING HORSE CHESTNUTS

- If a player intentionally moves their horse chestnut, the striker gets two shots.
- If the strings tangle, the first player to call "Strings!" gets an extra shot.
- If a striker hits a horse chestnut so hard it goes round in a full circle—known as a "round the world"—then they get an extra shot.
- If a player drops their horse chestnut or has it knocked out of their hand by the striker then the striker can shout "Stamps!" and jump on it, but only if the horse chestnut owner hasn't already shouted "No stamps!"

MISSION ACCOMPLISHED

I verify that on this date .... I created champion horse chestnuts with my Commando Dad.

Signed:

FOX AND HARE

Mission brief

- **Ground**: woodland or forest big enough to hide in—lots of trees and bushes to provide cover and concealment
- **Situation:** in the woods, we have predators (the fox) and prey (the hare)
- **Mission:** to track and catch your prey
- **Skills**: teamwork, communication, predator–prey connection

MISSION KEY

$ $ $ $ $ AGES 4+

KIT LIST:

- Sticks found on the forest floor

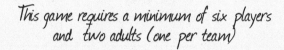

This game requires a minimum of six players and two adults (one per team)

INSTRUCTIONS:

This introduces your troopers to the link in nature between predators and prey:

- The predator is the animal that hunts and eats other animals.
- The prey is the animal that is eaten.

An example of this is the fox and the hare—the hare, which is the fox's prey, is always trying to survive, but then so is the fox! In nature, everything is about survival.

1 **Divide the troopers into two teams.** Team 1 are the predators and Team 2 are the prey (teams will get to swap roles, so everyone gets to play both roles).

2 **Team 2 prey must find a place in the woods to hide from the Team 1 predators,** who will come in search of them.

3 **The prey decide which direction they might want to head off in** and where they might hide—they then are given 5 minutes to collect sticks to use for their direction arrows, then 15 minutes to place them down and hide all together.

4 When the prey head off, they **place the arrows on the ground** so they are easy to see, but they don't lead all the way to their hiding spot—the track finishes with an "X" placed about 15 m (50 ft) away from their location.

5 **After 15 minutes, the predators set off.** They look for the signs left by their prey—just as they would do in the natural world.

6 **They follow the arrows until they reach the "X" mark.** They start to search the area together (without splitting up) to see if they can find their prey.

7 If the predators find the prey, they have won.

8 If the prey can avoid being seen and the predators pass them by, they can jump up and shout "We outfoxed you!" and they win.

9 Regardless of who wins, **both teams then return to the rally point and swap roles**.

10 Then the hunt can begin once again!

MISSION ACCOMPLISHED

I verify that on this date .... I tracked and caught my prey with my Commando Dad.

Signed:

NAPPING BEAR

Mission brief

- **Ground**: the forest, woods or any outdoor space
- **Situation**: the big, bad bear will wake up soon to eat
- **Mission**: to steal the bear's food without waking her
- **Skills**: stalking, silent moving, listening

MISSION KEY

$ $ $ $ AGES 4+

KIT LIST:

- Scarf or blindfold

- Object to be the bear's food, such as an apple

INSTRUCTIONS:

1 **All players link hands to make a circle,** then carefully walk backwards to make an even bigger one, before they sit down. If there aren't many troopers, let hands go so you still get a nice big circle.

2 **Choose one trooper to be the bear.** The bear sits in the middle of the circle.

3 **Give the bear some food**—it can be any object, but something a bear (and a trooper) might eat, like an apple, is a nice idea.

4 **The bear places the food down next to them** and has a short nap (Commando Dad puts a blindfold on the bear).

5 **Remind the troopers to keep very still and quiet,** so as not to wake the napping bear.

6 Once all is quiet, **Commando Dad can pick an intruder** who has to try and get the food.

7 **The bear has to listen very carefully for the greedy intruder,** and reach out and touch them before they get the food.

8 If the bear successfully grabs the intruder, they get to choose to remain as the bear, or they can choose another trooper to become the bear.

9 If the bear's food gets stolen by the intruder, then they can either become the bear or choose someone else.

MISSION ACCOMPLISHED

I verify that on this date .... I played napping bear with my Commando Dad.

Signed:

TWIG TOWERS

Mission brief

- **Ground**: forest floor with lots of sticks
- **Situation**: a calm day
- **Mission**: you need to build a sturdy tower that is taller than your competitors
- **Skills**: team work, problem solving, construction

MISSION KEY

$ $ $ $ $ AGES 5+

KIT LIST:

- Sticks (see instructions below for details)

You can play this game with individuals or as a team.

Building a freestanding tower:

To be successful, the troopers will need to create a tower that is wider and heavier at its base than at the top. You can start to help them think about this by asking them if they know of any towers; for example, Blackpool Tower, the Eiffel Tower or the Leaning Tower of Pisa. Once you are talking about a triangle shape with a wide bottom, ask them if they know of any other large, triangular structures that have stood the test of time—the pyramids of Egypt being the most obvious examples of this.

INSTRUCTIONS:

1. This is a game of two rounds. In round one, each individual or team is given **10 minutes to collect as many sticks as they can.**

2. **The team with the most sticks wins this round,** but you must make sure that both teams have roughly the same amount before tower construction begins. Do this by deploying all troopers to collect more sticks.

3. In round two, **troopers are given 15–20 minutes to build the tallest tower** or structure they can. It must be freestanding, i.e. nothing else is used to assist in keeping it up.

4. **Commando Dad decides the winner** and the decision is final.

MISSION ACCOMPLISHED

I verify that on this date .... I built a sturdy twig tower with my Commando Dad.

Signed:

GHOST WALK

Mission brief

- **Ground:** woods, forest or park
- **Situation**: woodland animals need to move with stealth and in silence. Can you do the same?
- **Mission**: to move through the woods without being heard
- **Skills:** stalking, animal imitation, body control

AGES 4+

KIT LIST:

- Blindfold for ghost hunter
- Whistle (if you don't have one, you can clap your hands)

You and your trooper can do this activity together, but it is even more fun when troopers are paired up.

INSTRUCTIONS:

1 **Explain how animals like foxes move through the woods very quietly,** lightly, slowly and stealthily so that they don't alert their prey. In the army, this is called "ghost walking." Give the troopers an example of you ghost walking and let them practise:

- From a standing position, remain perfectly still for 30 seconds.

- Take a step that should take another 30 seconds to complete—slowly raise your foot and smoothly move it forward, carefully looking ahead to see where to place it so as not to make a noise.

- Place your foot down, heel first, and roll onto the outside of your foot till your whole foot is down and taking the weight of your body. Repeat this slow, steady ghost walk.

2 **After practising, pair troopers up into ghosts and ghost hunters** and ask them to find a little area for the ghost hunt to take place.

3 **Blindfold the ghost hunters.** If there's more than one pair playing, give them a team name or number as you will need to alert them when the game begins.

4 The ghost can then move about 10 m (30 ft) away from their hunter and indicate to Commando Dad that they're ready to go (thumbs up is a good one).

5 **Commando Dad blows a whistle (or claps his hands)** and calls the name or

201

number of the team to let them know the game has started. He cannot be standing next to the ghost when he does this!

6 Ghosts begin their ghoulish journey and hunters use their sense of hearing to locate them.

7 If they reach the ghost hunter undetected, and touch their arm, they win.

8 If the ghost hunter hears them and can locate them by pointing and shouting "You're busted!" then the ghost hunter wins.

9 When the ghost is busted, players can swap over. If the ghost catches the hunter, the team decides if they swap or continue on in their roles.

MISSION ACCOMPLISHED

I verify that on this date .... I learned about ghost-walking and stealth with my Commando Dad.

Signed:

GLOSSARY

Base camp: Commando Dad and the unit's home.

Grommet: Metal rings lining a small hole at the edge of a tarp to accommodate the attachment of cords or bungees to the tarp.

Ground: Where a mission will take place.

In the field: Whenever Commando Dad and the unit are away from home.

Mess tin: A portable saucepan that is used for cooking while out and about by campers and the military.

Paracord: This is a lightweight thin nylon rope which can be used as a general purpose utility cord.

Rally point: A place designated by Commando Dad where his unit moves to reassemble and reorganize. All troopers must know where the rally point is, just in case they become separated from the unit, or Commando Dad calls them back.

Recce: Short for reconnaissance, a mission to obtain information.

SOP: Standard Operating Procedures; the normal, acknowledged way of doing things

Sortie: The dispatch of the unit; used to describe a trip away from base camp.

Squared away: Everything organized and in the right place and ready for an adventure.

Tarp: A sheet of heavy waterproof material that is used as a protective cover.

Troopers: The children that are taking part in the Forest School Adventures.

Unit: Family. Includes your own children and those you are caring for, parents and other carers.

USEFUL RESOURCES

 KNIVES AND THE LAW

Activities in this book may require you to use a saw or a knife. In these circumstances, the knife is a tool and should be treated as such. As with any other potentially dangerous tool, it should only be handled by you. If you have limited or no experience of using a knife for outdoor crafts, make sure you understand how to use it safely when you buy it. Make sure you know the right knives to use in the right situation. For advice on the safe use of knives, you can ask the shop assistant when you purchase your knife, or ideally sign up for a bushcraft course, where they will teach you all you need to know about knife safety.

Depending on your State and locality, certain types of knives might be considered illegal weapons. It is your responsibility to familiarize yourself with the laws in your jurisdiction. If you have any questions or concerns, contact your local law enforcement.

COMMANDO DAD'S NOTES

COMMANDO DAD'S NOTES